MW01679859

GOD'S WORD
day upon day

God's Word Day upon Day: Devotions for Every Season of Your Life offers a fresh method of developing a heart for God. When God's words blend into our lives, we grow spiritually. This devotional takes a unique approach by using the four seasons and the seasons of our lives to help us grow spiritually. This is an approach that respects the situation in life that one is in, and then directs that person to God. Start applying scripture to your life today with this wonderful resource.

—Dr. Chris Cobb, Pastor,
Western Hills Baptist Church

If you want to be encouraged every day of the year, read and record your reflections through the devotions in *God's Word Day upon Day: Devotions for Every Season of Your Life.* It is truly a breath of God for your life.

—Dr. Don E. McQueen, D.D, BA,
Behavioral Science

In this collection of devotionals, the sisters have created a wonderful spiritual tool for daily use. No matter where or when you start, God's Word leaps off the pages and into practical daily application for a better, more fulfilling life. Dive in! Commune! Grow! *God's Word Day upon Day: Devotions for Every Season of Your Life* holds His abundant blessings.

—Sandy Richardson, editor, ghostwriter,
and author of *The Girl Who Ate Chicken Feet*

GOD'S WORD

day upon day

Kathleen Jones, Maureen Eubank
& Peggy Seay

GOD'S WORD
day upon day

DEVOTIONS FOR EVERY SEASON OF YOUR LIFE

TATE PUBLISHING & *Enterprises*

Published by Tate Publishing & Enterprises, LLC
127 E. Trade Center Terrace | Mustang, Oklahoma 73064 USA
1.888.361.9473 | www.tatepublishing.com

Tate Publishing is committed to excellence in the publishing industry. The company reflects the philosophy established by the founders, based on Psalm 68:11,
"The Lord gave the word and great was the company of those who published it."

Cover design by Amber Gulilat
Interior design by Stephanie Woloszyn

Published in the United States of America

ISBN: 978-1-61566-824-3
1. Religion / Christian Life / Devotional
2. Religion / Christian Life / Spiritual Growth
10.01.25

dedication

To each reader. As you pass through your personal "seasons of life," we pray you will reflect on God's Words, using this devotional, *God's Word Day upon Day.* We pray your relationship with Jesus is enriched by these words and may you enjoy each page with the love and care they are presented.

acknowledgments

The Trinity—God the Father, God the Son, and God the Holy Spirit—for without your presence in our lives and the grace that only you can give, this work would not have made it to fruition. Praise your holy name, El Shaddai.

Sandy Richardson, editor: What a blessing to work with Sandy. Her knowledge and expertise helped to make this work become a calm reality. Thank you, Sandy!

table of contents

PART I

spring

PART II

summer

PART III

autumn

PART IV

winter

preface

What an adventurous mission this book has been! I say *mission,* because wherever God plants us becomes our mission field. I say *adventurous,* because when we sisters started this project, we had three things: (1) our trust in God's nudging, (2) minute experience writing manuals for the different companies for which we worked, and (3) our belief that staying close to Jesus Christ means staying in God's Word daily.

To begin our trek into *God's Word Day upon Day: Devotions for Every Season of Your Life* wilderness, we started a Web site: www.sistersletstalk.com. At first we were unsure devotions on the Web site was God's plan for us. But we soon saw the need as more and more individuals visited the Web site, even though we didn't have advertising for it in any way. It didn't take long before we felt the Lord nudging us to take one more step on the path of His plan. God urged us to create something all people could use no matter their place or position. We knew that whatever He was leading us to do had to be useful to all, give the opportunity for each person to grow from their own personal experiences, and had to provide directions from God for each daily life it touched. There also had to be an opportunity for personal reflection for what God might be saying.

We believe life is made up of daily situations, which we do not always feel equipped to handle. Many times these situations come about by our own daily choices and decisions. Some things we experience only once in a lifetime, and some things we struggle with day after day. No matter the situation or trial, God always has a plan for each of us. His plan requires that we turn to Him for every decision we make—no matter if that decision is only for what we are to eat today or a decision that will affect the world—we are to consider His divine ways. There is but one way to draw close enough to Him and to hear His pleas for our lives, and that is to know Him. Since we cannot look Him in the face to have a conversation, we get to know Him through reading His Word and bowing ourselves to Him in prayer.

As you go through each week of these devotions, may God bless you with renewed strength for your every trial. By God's mercy, may you begin to know that He and His Word can be relied upon for every situation. May you begin to know today that your deepening relationship with Christ better equips you for what this world puts in your path.

GOD'S WORD
day upon day

DEVOTIONS FOR EVERY SEASON OF YOUR LIFE

PART I

spring

Bloom into your life with Christ

SPRING

One step forward, two steps back.
The harder I try, the more I lack.
How did I get in the worldly maze?
Is this forever or just a phase?

The road ahead,
He has firmly chosen.
Before this moment,
My path I had frozen.

By His Words, a blossom begins.
By His Love, confidence
And encouragement He sends.

Each of His days
Grows strength and beauty.
All to me, He has freely given
And never attached any duty.

—*Kathleen J. Jones*—

The spring of life finds you filled with confidence and encouragement. God responds by growing you to His understandings. Through your self-growth of changed attitudes and life outlooks, your very own garden begins to bloom.

He Gives Us Hope for Every Day

God has provided a glimpse into church beginnings in 1 and 2 Corinthians. Paul was able to communicate with the Corinthians—through his letters—on their various needs. It is a wonderful thing to open an old letter and be reminded of the happenings of that time. We often remember good times and bad. The same is true for Paul's letters. You will find happy and sad, good and bad, things that need correcting and things for which God must be very proud. There was life in Corinth, just as there is life today in your city, town, or community.

SUNDAY:

Blessed be the God and Father of our Lord Jesus Christ, the Father of mercies and God of all comfort.

2 Corinthians 1:3 (NKJV)

Start your week by lifting your arms and thoughts high to the Father of Jesus Christ and *you.* Praise Him with your words and thoughts today for tender mercies He has provided in the past and has set aside for your future. He is our greatest comfort in every situation. Thank Him that you don't have to look for anyone else because He is always there for you.

Write to God about your hope for today and begin turning the soil in your relationship growth with God.

MONDAY:

> Who comforts us in all our tribulation, that we may be able to comfort those who are in any trouble with the comfort with which we ourselves are comforted by God.
>
> 2 Corinthians 1:4 (NKJV)

In recent years, several movies carried the "pass-it-on" theory. God is the author of this theory. He gives to us willingly whenever we are in need. First, thank Him for His comfort in all situations, just because you call to Him. Second, "*pass it on.*" Find someone who needs comforting. Offer them your compassion; then offer them God's. If that person will allow, pray together to the Father to ask for His continued comfort. If your joint prayers are not wanted, find a secret place and pray to the Father for that person.

Lift your praise to Him. Then list those things you might be able to use the "pass it on" plan with today. You will be planting your seeds for growth with God.

TUESDAY:

For we walk by faith, not by sight.

2 Corinthians 5:7 (NKJV)

No matter your personality, walking by faith is not an easy task. It is a learned experience. Today, give Him thanks that you can confidently walk by faith. Confess to Him any time you might have questioned how far you had to walk before He gave a definitive direction. Next, close your eyes, and imagine all the beautiful places walking with Him in faith can take you. Lastly, tell Him of His majesty and glory for deciding your walk and the path(s).

List some of the paths He has chosen for you. Your seeds to grow your relationship with God have begun to spring forward.

WEDNESDAY:

> Therefore, if anyone is in Christ, he is a new creation; old things have passed away; behold, all things have become new.
>
> 2 Corinthians 5:17 (NKJV)

Ever had an article of clothing you just loved? You loved the way it fit, the colors, the style—just everything about it! Then it got old and very ragged looking, because you wore it and washed it so often. Nothing could be done except to throw it away. Life with Jesus Christ is nothing like life with that garment. We don't have to worry about too many wash and dry cycles. He is there for you *now* and *tomorrow*. Ask Him to wash away all the dirtiness in your life. He will throw it into the ocean, never to be seen again. By calling to Him daily, your life can be refreshed. He loves you so much; He makes your life new each time you come to Him.

Write your thanks to Him for your newness. You havc now come to taking the weeds from around your garden.

THURSDAY:

> For God is not the author of confusion but of peace, as in all the churches of saints.
>
> 1 Corinthians 14:33 (NKJV)

Our days are filled with decisions. Most choices are made without realizing we have made a judgment call. We often do not call upon the Lord, because we feel He is too busy, or we are too busy and do not want to wait for the answer. For one day, call upon the Father for every decision. See if it doesn't release you and give you peace. Tell Him thank you for all the answers He is going to give you, even those for which you are not aware.

List a few of your daily decisions He can decide for you.

FRIDAY:

Let all things be done decently and in order.

1 Corinthians 14:40 (NKJV)

Usually, our hope begins to wane when life just keeps coming at us. It seems we must deal with new trials daily. Confusion comes when we must add new trials to the old ones. But God is not a God of disorder. His creations are always orderly. Ask the Father today to restructure your plan or make you a new one. Let Him tell you what is important to get done today. Praise Him for setting up all your tomorrows. Let Him make all your lists and any timetables you feel must be met.

Try listing your daily duties in an order of importance and time needed.

SATURDAY:

e have this treasure in earthen vessels, that the excel-
e of the power may be of God and not of us.

2 Corinthians 4:7 (NKJV)

.e are clay pots. We will wear out, break, and get old. But God never will! Cast all your hopes on Him. Let Him bear all your burdens. Sing praises to your Father in heaven, who will cover your every need, make all your decisions, hold you tight from every harm, and love you through each day with His promises. He was, He is, and He will always be your El Shaddai, your God Almighty.

Look back through this week and list some of the hopes God has already answered. Your relationship with God has come to full bloom, now you only have to keep the weeds from overtaking it.

Lips of Love

There are times we get together and have "friendly" discussions—oh we don't mean anything by what we are discussing, we are just being silly or having private fun. But is it really private? If the truth be known, is it really fun or friendly? Satan makes sin appear simple, which is why we must be on our guard. Practice having "Lips of Love" this week as you learn what God's Word has to say about friendly discussions.

SUNDAY:

> Let no corrupt communication proceed out of your mouth, but that, which is good to the use of edifying, that it may minister grace unto the hearers.
>
> Ephesians 4:29 (KJV)

The word *corrupt* means evil, and evil means harmful. But if evil means harmful, ouch! How many times have you been sitting around and casually discussing someone? Could your words be construed as harmful? Could you be evil? Maybe the words you speak are true, but does that mean it is okay to discuss someone else, especially when that person is not present. Perhaps, you're saying to yourself, "But I'd tell them to their face." Do you really mean that? This scripture does not qualify that our harmful conversations are true or false. It says let *no* harmful communication proceed. What is harmful then? Suppose someone's child or parent heard what was being said. How would that person feel hearing your words, even if those words were truthful? The words could still cause harm. When you consider the definition of harmful, your communication can take on a whole new meaning; journal your reflective prayer below, and commit to the Lord that you will not let corrupt communication proceed out of your mouth.

MONDAY:

> Which is good to the use of edifying.
>
> Ephesians 4:29b (KJV)

The verse above tells us that what does proceed from our mouths is to lift others up or to educate others. *Edifying* means to instruct or improve. If your communication does not teach or encourage to make better then you are not following the biblical principal of today's verse. List ways you can encourage or guide others in your daily walk.

TUESDAY:

That it may minister grace unto the hearers.

Ephesians 4:29c (KJV)

Grace refers to a pleasing and admiring quality. How many times have your words gone awry? During those times you may have been disgruntled with a spouse, a child, another family member, a friend, a boss, or a coworker. Your words were not comforting others. Stop and consider what others hear from you. List below ways you can change your words to reassure or support others.

WEDNESDAY:

Let your speech be always with grace.

Colossians 4:6a (KJV)

This verse uses the words *always* and *grace*. The word *always* tends to trip me up. God tells us we are to "strive" for mastery over sin. God knows you are not perfect, but ask yourself if you are really trying. The word *grace* should remind you that Christ gave you eternity when you did not deserve it. Today, strive to fill your speech with grace constantly. Write your prayer below asking God to guide your words at all times.

THURSDAY:

But speaking the truth in love.

Ephesians 4:15 (KJV)

If you desire to have "Lips of Love," this verse should reign in your heart. Being truthful and honest does not mean your delivery has to be harsh and hurtful. Godly love will change the attitude in which you speak. Reflect below how your times of truthfulness can be given in love and affection.

FRIDAY:

Let your conversation be without covetousness.

Hebrews 13:5a (KJV)

When we consider our general conversations, let us not find that we long for things that do not belong to us. The Ten Commandments instruct us of this, and in this verse, we are told not to even discuss desiring something or someone. The rest of the verse tells us to be content with what we have. *Why?* Because Christ will never leave us or forsake us, He is all we need, so what does that leave to crave? Learning to totally rely on Jesus can teach us the right conversation. List below items you think you may be wanting and ask God to work in your life regarding these items.

SATURDAY:

Be won by the conversation of the wives.

1 Peter 3:1b (KJV)

I pray you can take this one-step further and see who we can "win" by our conversation. The verse above shows us that our conversations can win others for Christ. A positive and happy verbal life can cause others to ask why or how you can speak with the love and affection you show. These words can show others the love of Christ. List ways you can alter your speech and ask God to give you those "Lips of Love."

Passion Week

Passion Week begins with Palm Sunday and was the last week Jesus walked the earth as the Son of Man. It is important in growing your relationship to God you begin to know how the Old Testament and the New Testament work together. By using both Old and New you will gain an even deeper relationship to the Father and the Son.

> Rejoice greatly, O daughter of Zion! Shout, O daughter of Jerusalem! Behold, your King is coming to you; He is just and having salvation, lowly and riding on a donkey, a colt, the foal of a donkey.
>
> Zechariah 9:9 (NKJV)

SUNDAY:

> Now when they drew near Jerusalem, to Bethphage and Bethany, at the Mount of Olives, He sent two of His disciples; and He said to them, "Go into the village opposite you; And as soon as you have entered it you will find a colt tied, on which no one has sat, Loose it and bring it."
>
> Mark 11:1–2 (NKJV)

List the things Zechariah said would occur and those that actually happened in Mark.

MONDAY:

> All this was done that it might be fulfilled which was spoken by the prophet saying: "Tell the daughter of Zion, behold, your King is coming to you, lowly, and sitting on a donkey, a colt, the foal of a donkey." So the disciples went and did as Jesus commanded them."
>
> Matthew 21:4–6 (NKJV)

List the things Zechariah said would occur and those that actually happened in Matthew.

TUESDAY:

> And many spread their clothes on the road, and others cut down leafy branches from the trees and spread them on the road, then those who went before and those who followed cried out, saying: "Hosanna! Blessed is He who comes in the name of the Lord! Blessed is the kingdom of our father David that comes in the name of the Lord! Hosanna in the highest!
>
> Mark 11:8–10 (NKJV)

Jesus was from the Davidic lineage. Jesus came to earth because God asked Him to bring us salvation. He also came as our King. "Hosanna in the highest" is equal to saying Jesus our Messianic Deliverer.

Write how the people honored their King in Mark. How should we honor Him today?

WEDNESDAY:

> Save now, I pray, O Lord; O Lord, I pray, send now prosperity, blessed is he who comes in the name of the Lord! We have blessed you from the house of the Lord.
>
> Psalm 118: 25–26 (NKJV)

The Psalmist knew when the deliverer came there would be prosperity and blessing for all. The one who was to come would be called blessed and be straight from God. You too can be assured Jesus is your deliverer and the called blessed from God.

What has Psalms told us that is also said in Zechariah? Also remind yourself what He is bringing.

THURSDAY:

> And when He had come into Jerusalem, all the city was moved, saying, "Who is this?" So the multitudes said, "This is Jesus, the prophet from Nazareth of Galilee."
>
> Matthew 21:10–11 (NKJV)

From the beginning of time God planned for Jesus to enter the city with greatness. True, He did not enter as a king but instead on a donkey. His road was not paved with gold but instead palm branches. God has a plan. He sees it one way, but we often expect it another. To grow your relationship you must see things with God's eyes not your own.

How did the multitude know who this was that was coming? Hint: it is in Zechariah.

FRIDAY:

> And some of the Pharisees called to Him from the crowd, "Teacher, rebuke Your disciples." But He answered and said to them, "I tell you that if these should keep silent, the stones would immediately cry out."
>
> Luke 19:39–40 (NKJV)

The Pharisees were jealous of the adoration Jesus was receiving. Jesus was so close to His Father that He knew what God had planned. Jesus was confident enough in his relationship that He wasn't boasting but instead saying what God had for Him to say.

Write how you will respond when your King returns or if He should enter your city.

SATURDAY:

> His disciples did not understand these things at first: but when Jesus was glorified, then they remembered that these things were written about Him and that they had done these things to Him.
>
> John 12:16 (NKJV)

Sometimes it is very hard to read God's words and know exactly how He wants us to respond. Many times you might not remember what you read just after you have read it. But God will bring it back to mind when the time is right for you. That is why it is so important to keep reading His word daily.

List some things that have happened relating to your relationship with God that maybe you didn't understand "at first."

Who is in Control?

Some of us think we need to be in control of what is going on around us. We work both inside and outside the home. If we can be all, we must be able to be in control of our own lives.

SUNDAY:

> Then the word of the Lord came to him: "This man will not be your heir, but a son coming from your own body will be your heir."
>
> Genesis 15:4 (NKJV)

> So she said to Abram, "The Lord has kept me from having children. Go, sleep with my maidservant; perhaps I can build a family through her."
>
> Genesis 16:2 (NKJV)

How many times have we received a word from God, but we felt, He was just taking too long to fulfill what He said He would do? We then decide, "I am going to go ahead and help Him achieve what He said." Sarai moved ahead, and it was not what God had in mind. To achieve *His* results, we must *wait for Him.*

Remind yourself of something you heard from God but didn't wait for Him to make come to fruition.

MONDAY:

> When Abram was ninety-nine years old, the LORD appeared to him and said, 'I am God Almighty; walk before me and be blameless. I will confirm my covenant between me and you and will greatly increase your numbers.
>
> Genesis 17:1–2 (NKJV)

God had a plan. Sarai thought she would help Him along with His plan. It did not turn out the way God had in mind. But God's real plan did. He planned to increase Abram's numbers greatly. All Sarai and Abram had to do was wait for God's plan to be fulfilled in God's time. Do not be a Sarai when you are given a word from God. His answer will come to pass. Wait on Him to fulfill *His plan.*

Write some things you are waiting for God to answer in His time.

TUESDAY:

> For a while he stayed in Gerar, and there Abraham said of his wife Sarah, "She is my sister." Then Abimelech King of Gerar sent for Sarah and took her."
>
> Genesis 20:1b–2 (NKJV)

Abraham had decided Abimelech would kill him and take Sarah. Abraham decided to take matters into his own hands by telling a lie. It was after all "just a little lie." She really was his sister. But even little lies show we are not trusting God. Fear feeds dishonesty.

What fears may have caused you to not face the truth of a situation you found yourself in?

WEDNESDAY:

> Now Abimelech had not gone near her, so he said, "Lord, will you destroy an innocent nation? Did he not say to me, 'She is my sister,' and didn't she also say, 'He is my brother?' I have done this with a clear conscience and clean hands."
>
> Genesis 20:4–5 (NKJV)

God knew what Abraham and Sarah had done. They did not trust God to keep them safe as they traveled. Trust and do not fear what may lie ahead. If we are following God's path, there is nothing to fear.

How has your trust in God kept you from being fearful in times of need?

THURSDAY:

> So the sisters sent word to Jesus, "Lord, the one you love is sick."
>
> John 11:3 (NKJV)

> Yet when he heard that Lazarus was sick, he stayed where he was two more days.
>
> John 11:6 (NKJV)

Mary and Martha called out for Jesus to come now saying, "Our brother is sick; he needs your healing hands." When we call to Jesus, do we demand his answer immediately? These verses tell us it is God's timing, and not ours, which Jesus follows.

Remind yourself of a time you called to God demanding His intervention immediately. How did it work out?

FRIDAY:

> When he heard this, Jesus said, "This sickness will not end in death. No, it is for God's glory so that God's Son may be glorified through it."
>
> John 11:4 (NKJV)

At times, we may think and feel that if God does not act at the very moment we ask, He is not who He says He is. When we ask and God answers immediately, who are we inclined to think was in control? We may tend to believe it was because "we asked" that the answer was immediate; therefore, we were in control of when the answer was given. This scripture tells us that Jesus waited to answer, because He was glorifying God. Give God His glory by waiting for His answer.

Write today asking His forgiveness for demands you might have made in the past.

SATURDAY:

> But with loud shouts they insistently demanded that he be crucified, and their shouts prevailed.
>
> Luke 23:23 (NKJV)

> Why do you look for the living among the dead? He is not here; he has risen! Remember how he told you, while he was still with you in Galilee: "The Son of Man must be delivered into the hands of sinful men, be crucified and on the third day be raised again."
>
> Luke 24:5b–7 (NKJV)

We need to allow God to be in control. The people thought they were in control of killing Jesus, but God was in control. Jesus was crucified, and He arose for us, according to God's plan. Let go of the control and allow God to show the way.

Tell God today how thankful you are He was and is in control. Without it you would not have a Savior.

For Sale

In the paper, in the front yard, on the Internet, and registered with all the multiple listing services are houses waiting to be purchased by new owners. As I drove along, I noticed the signs and advertisements everywhere. "Why did they jump out at me so?" I asked. The Holy Spirit and I were in our normal "ride-home-from-the-office" conversation.

So when the "For Sale" signs continued to draw my attention, I simply had to ask myself, "Are you *for sale?*"

"Of course not," I answered!

Then, as He always does, God gave me a closer look. He will do the same for you with this week's devotions.

SUNDAY:

> If we confess our sins, he is faithful and just to forgive us our sins, and to cleanse us from all unrighteousness.
>
> 1 John 1:9 (KJV)

Are you "on the market?" If you have salvation, that is absolutely wonderful. But did you know that, even with salvation, we still sin? God's forgiveness is necessary everyday. Forgiveness should not be requested in generalities. Be specific as to your sins. And here is the clincher: you have to "confess." To be sure you do not allow yourselves even the appearance of being for sale, stay in a right relationship with Christ. Satan is going to have his "realtors" searching for new property. Look at yourself this week. Have you asked for forgiveness? If not, ask Him today, and turn toward a right relationship with Him. Write your prayer below.

MONDAY:

> I call heaven and earth to record this day against you, that I have set before you life and death, blessing and cursing: therefore choose life, that both thou and thy seed may live: That thou mayest love the LORD thy God, and that thou mayest obey his voice, and that thou mayest cleave unto him: for he is thy life, and the length of thy days: that thou mayest dwell in the land which the LORD sware unto thy fathers, to Abraham, to Isaac, and to Jacob, to give them.
>
> Deuteronomy 30:19–20 (KJV)

May I submit to you that, unless you obey His voice, you will most definitely be putting yourself "on the market" for sin? Sin creeps up on you, little by little, piece by piece. Then, *Bam!* Sin is in your face, and you are entering into a precontract. Hearing and obeying God's voice will keep you from signing on the dotted line of sin. Take some time today to read His Word and *"cleave unto Him: for He is thy life."* Reflect below ways that you can keep yourself off the market of sin.

TUESDAY:

> Create in me a clean heart, O God; and renew a right spirit within me.
>
> Psalm 51:10 (KJV)

"My heart is clean," may be your first thought, and it's true. God created a clean heart for you, but could there be things that have shaded your heart to gray? Look deeper into this verse and to "the spirit within." God is not just about creating a clean heart. He wants to renew the spirit within you daily. He is asking today, "Are you for sale"? List ways below you can renew your spirit and your relationship with Christ.

WEDNESDAY:

Jesus Christ himself being the chief corner stone.

Ephesians 2:20b (KJV)

When purchasing a building, a major concern is the structural support. No matter the building material, the cornerstone is the most important support. Put some blocks together. If the corner block is not secured, the blocks tumble down. Our lives are like that without "the chief cornerstone." We tumble and wobble; we are out of line and not level. Let Christ be your *chief* cornerstone, and you will have sure support. Do you have a sure support? Use the lines below to thank God for giving you a foundation you can always rely upon.

THURSDAY:

They allure through the lust of the flesh.

2 Peter 2:18b (KJV)

To sell a piece of property requires taking pictures and writing ads that appeal, so the property will attract buyers. To *allure* is to exert a very powerful and often dangerous attraction on someone. Satan uses charming schemes. If you are not careful, you, too, will be drawn by Satan's dangers. It happens when you hang out with wrong crowds, "discuss" someone, watch the wrong programs and movies, and listen to wrong music and wrong advice. 2 Peter 2 tells of false prophets and the results of listening to them. All of these are easy to do, if you are denying the Lord your God. What is attracting you today?

FRIDAY:

God is love.

1 John 4:8b (KJV)

When you find the right property, your heart and soul are filled as you exclaim, "Oh, I love it!" Today, think on the *One* that is love and how much *He* loves you. Ask yourself, "Am I for sale?" Look to the world, and say, "I am not for sale! God has purchased me, and He is a permanent resident in my life." List ways you can see your permanent resident living in your life.

SATURDAY:

> For God so loved the world, that he gave his only begotten Son, that whosoever believeth in him should not perish, but have everlasting life.
>
> John 3:16 (KJV)

Yesterday we determined we have been purchased by a permanent resident and are *not* for sale. Today's verse tells us we have everlasting life. We have the Son of God in our hearts forever! He resides within, and Satan knows this. Satan tries to allure and cause you to forget *Who* lives in your heart. The God who is love gives you the strength to stand up and say, "No, I am not for sale!" Think on this, as you pass those *For Sale* signs in the future. Whisper a prayer of praise and thanksgiving. You have a permanent resident.

Jesus and the Seven “Re”s of Us

Everybody wants a redo. Our God is a God of seconds, thirds, and even more chances. He allows us to make our mistakes, and if we desire, we can ask for a “redo.” As I thought about the number of changes and overs God has allowed in my life I began to review the “re” concept—words like regarding pertaining to, and on the subject of. Many words in our language begin with “re” but do not actually reflect this principal. To keep the principal of “re” on your mind, I have prepared a week of words that begin with “re.” As you go through each day, reflect on the word and how the word concerns your life.

SUNDAY:

> For everyone that asks receives; he who seeks finds; and to him who knocks, the door will be opened.
>
> Matthew 7:8 (NIV)

He receives you. He takes you from where you were and brings you back to Him. Jesus delivers you to the Father, and the Father receives you. Do you hear the knocking? He is waiting for you to open the door, so He can receive you.

When you open the door to the knocking, thank God for receiving you. Use the lines below to tell Him what it means to you to be received by Him.

MONDAY:

> O Israel, put your hope in the LORD, for with the LORD is unfailing love and with him is full redemption. He himself will redeem Israel from all their sins."
>
> Psalm 130:7–8 (NIV)

He redeems you. *Redeem* means to pay for the sins of humanity with death on the cross. Christ paid the highest cost anyone could pay for you. To Him, you are worth the price of His death on the cross. Believe and know, that to Him, you are worthy of His death. Use your name in the place of Israel in the above verse. It will bring it home to you.

Write out your prayer thanking Him for redeeming you.

TUESDAY:

> Though your sins are like scarlet, they shall be as white as snow; though they are red as crimson, they shall be like wool.
>
> Isaiah 1:18b (NIV)

The Lord removes your sins. The scripture tells you when your sins are removed you become spotless, cleaner than you can become by taking a scrubbing hot bath. Something that begins as scarlet cannot become white by scrubbing the red out of it, not even by bleaching it can it become as the whiteness of snow. Only the hand of God can take away the sin and clean you up. God creates a gleaming new you when you confess your sins. Allow *Him* to remove your sins today. How glorious is His Word!

Tell Him of the sins removed to make you white as snow.

WEDNESDAY:

> They will rebuild the ancient ruins and restore the places long devastated; they will renew the ruined cities that have been devastated for generations.
>
> Isaiah 61:4 (NIV)

God restores you. Have you ever seen how an old piece of furniture is restored? With loving hands, the scratches are removed one-by-one. You can become like old furniture—scarred and broken, devastated by the trials of life. God will restore you with loving hands and give you a life renewed.

Do you see the scarred and broken pieces being restored? Tell God about them, and thank Him for restoring you.

THURSDAY:

> Yet, O LORD, you are our Father. We are the clay, you are the potter; we are all the work of your hand.
>
> Isaiah 64:8 (NIV)

The Father remolds you. You began as a child, and He remolds you into the most beautiful person you can become. Allow His hands to mold and remold you into the beautiful person He wants you to become.

Are you feeling beautiful yet? If you are, tell Him about it. If not, tell Him why you don't.

FRIDAY:

> Come and see what God has done, how awesome his works in man's behalf!
>
> Psalm 66:5 (NIV)

God refines you. Like a rock polished and buffed to reveal the jewel it can become, God refines you. Look in the mirror, and see His awesome work. As you continue in the changing process, He continues the improving process—refining you in small ways, making you pure. Through His refining, you become as a precious jewel.

You are becoming a precious jewel; it takes time for the jewel to be revealed. Write your thoughts on how the process is affecting you.

SATURDAY:

> "Behold, I am coming soon! My reward is with me, and I will give to everyone according to what he has done."
>
> Revelation 22:12 (NIV)

Jesus rewards you. You do the wrong, and He does the cleaning. Accepting Him as your savior is all you must do to receive eternity with Him. The gift you are given is a reward not the punishment you deserve. You are given the re-dos and the rewards.

Take today to write your praise to God for all your re-dos and your rewards.

Patience

I used to pray for my patience to grow. Then someone told me praying for patience is exactly what brings the tribulations we receive in life. God answers our prayers for patience by sending situations that demand it of us. I wasn't sure I believed exactly that, but I did quit praying for patience!

Instead, I went (where I should have gone in the first place) to God's Word(s) on patience. I pray you will use these scriptures. Contemplate them. Let God respond to you. Use your thought time this week to find how God wants you to increase your patience. I believe patience is one of the things God does want us to grow.

SUNDAY:

> But the fruit of the spirit is love, joy, peace, long suffering, kindness, goodness, faithfulness.
>
> Galatians 5:22 (NKJV)

Long suffering equals patience. Patience is a part of the fruits of the Spirit, and according to medical science, we are to have three fruit servings per day for a healthy body. Is patience on your menu today? True patience can only come about when we put all our trust in Jesus Christ.

What have you been called on to be patient about today? Trust it to the hand of your Lord and Savior. Tell Him about it now.

MONDAY:

> It is good that one should hope and wait quietly for the salvation of the Lord.
>
> Lamentations 3:26 (NKJV)

Hope and wait quietly equals patience. We are commanded to "wait quietly." The word *salvation* in this scripture can be thought of as being saved from a negative circumstance brought about because we did not wait on the Lord. Waiting quietly means we are to spend our time in prayer or talking it over with God. You will find talking over the waiting with friends often brings more anticipation. Talking it over with God brings serenity and deepens your trust in Him.

Talk a frustration over with Him today.

TUESDAY:

> Do not hasten in your spirit to be angry, for anger rests in the bosom of fools
>
> Ecclesiastes 7:9 (NKJV)

Many times our impatience brings us to the boiling point, making us *fools*. Ever been in a long line waiting and waiting and just as you come to the front someone stepped ahead of you? Bet you were more than just a little upset. Was your first reaction to say something witty but negative? Scripture says our first reaction should not be anger but love and patience. These are qualities that show an intimate relationship with God.

Write your scenario of how you should respond with Christ's attitude in a boiling point situation.

WEDNESDAY:

> Whatever things were written before, were written for our learning, that we through the patience and comfort of the Scriptures might have hope.
>
> Romans 15:4 (NKJV)

Seems odd to think we can gain hope through being patient. But the scriptures tell us exactly that. Patience is a learned attitude. How did you learn to read or write? You had to practice, practice, practice. So it is with patience. You will start with little things that annoy you and grow to have patience even when someone was just plain rude.

Ask God today what annoyance you can use to strengthen your patience and hope.

THURSDAY:

> Rest in the Lord, and wait patiently for Him; do not fret because of him who prospers in his way, because of the man who brings wicked schemes to pass.
>
> Psalm 37:7 (NKJV)

Know someone who got all they have through a scheme or by lying? Be assured God will answer this wickedness in a timely manner. Our thoughts should be on Him and not our neighbors, who have perhaps achieved goals through wicked schemes. You are not called on to judge the right or wrong of what someone has or even how they got it. You are called on to wait upon the Lord and His rewards for you. Remember, our time is not His time. He leads; we follow.

Use your journal to pray for someone you think might need to know Christ. Let Christ judge if their gains are ill gotten.

FRIDAY:

> I waited patiently for the Lord; and He inclined to me, and heard my cry.
>
> Psalm 40:1 (NKJV)

The most important part of patience is *waiting on the Lord.* There is only one way I know to wait patiently, and that is to continually lift it to God to bring what ever I am waiting on to His fruition. Many times I spend my day revisiting the same issue with God. I know there are some who believe we should only pray once about an issue. But I believe God wants to hear all our issues whenever we might have them on our mind. I believe my patience is shown to Him by trusting He will respond. By showing Him your patience, He will hear you and respond. If you can wait on the Lord, you have conquered patience.

Tell Him thank you today for hearing and responding every time you bring an issue to Him.

SATURDAY:

> We also glory in tribulations, knowing that tribulation produces perseverance; and perseverance, character; and character hope. Now hope does not disappoint, because the love of God has been poured out in our hearts by the Holy Spirit who was given to us.
>
> Romans 5:3–5 (NKJV)

And so we are back where we started. Praying for patience brings tribulation. So let us not pray for patience, but instead, let us look to our Father to supply. He will not only supply the patience we need, but everything else as well. He has already given us patience by supplying us His Son, Jesus Christ. We just need to stop and use (call on) the One Jesus left with us, the Holy Spirit.

Tell Him today how your relationship with Him has grown deeper this week.

Bundles to Burn

Spring is a wonderful time of year. I love the tulips and other bulb plants. Bradford Pear trees are abundant in the Southeast. I am not one with a "green thumb," but I enjoy the bounty of spring to the fullest. This week the devotion will focus on a parable from Matthew 13:24–30. I do not tire of hearing the first four words Jesus spoke in this parable: "The kingdom of Heaven …" Times are hard, it is true, but may I submit to you … the kingdom of heaven! Just thinking on those words give me a delight, and a soulful calm within the innermost part of me is my best attempt to express what happens within my being. Join me this week for a wonderful look into God's Holy Word.

SUNDAY:

> Another parable put he forth unto them, saying, the kingdom of heaven is likened unto a man which sowed good seed in his field:
>
> Matthew 13:24 (KJV)

Notice the colon at the end of this verse. A colon is used to divide distinct but related sentence components such as clauses in which the second elaborates on the first. This entire parable will relate back to the most important part … the kingdom of heaven. How could Jesus relate heaven to the disciples? How can he relate heaven to you? Human mind cannot comprehend the glory of it all. Yet Jesus takes time to explain a very important truth.

Using good seed is a vital part of a successful garden or harvest. The man in this parable has taken care to sow good seed in 'his' field. Do you take care and sow good seed? Have you been careless and just tossed a half-learned seed to the field? Consider these two questions today and ask Jesus to help you sow good seed.

MONDAY:

> But while men slept, his enemy came and sowed tares among the wheat, and went his way.
>
> Matthew 13:25 (KJV)

What goes on while you are sleeping? Unless you have a recorder going, how would you know? In this weeks parable we are shown one very huge fact: the enemy came! Once there he sowed tares (or weeds) then went his way. You too, can be sure the enemy is on his way. He will arrive, sow tares (disruptions and vitamin stealers), and then he (the enemy) will go his way. He does not care about the pain and havoc left in your life. You are, according to him, asleep. Your only recourse is to stay awake and alert. There may be times that you dose and even get weary. Look to Jesus for the strength you need to stay awake because you can be sure the enemy will sow tares in your life while you sleep.

TUESDAY:

> But when the blade was sprung up, and brought forth fruit then appeared the tares also.
>
> Matthew 13:26 (KJV)

The good seed brought forth fruit. *Then.* You press forward in the work of God, witnessing and striving for the mastery as God's Word tells you to do. Blades are beginning to make their way through the soil and spring up. Satan has left his mark ever so subtly—a tare here and a tare there. Small little weeds in your life are attempting to blend with the good seed. Do they blend in your life? Spend some time today and ask God to show you the tares in your life. Thank Him for helping you see the tares the enemy sowed and give you strength and wisdom to follow Christ.

WEDNESDAY:

> So the servants of the householder came and said unto him, Sir, didst not thou sow good seed in thy field? From whence then hath it tares?
>
> Matthew 13:27 (KJV)

Others are watching your every move. Could someone be saying, "Hey, she/he is suppose to be a Christian why is she/he _____ (fill in the blanks)." Even the things you do not notice in your own life, others will. God's Word says you are not to cause others to stumble in the law (Malachi 2:7–9) but you are to "study to show thyself approved unto God, a workman that needeth not to be ashamed, rightly dividing the word of truth" (2 Timothy 2:15). Is it time to get in the book, my friend? What do you need to change in your life to grow your relationship with him?

THURSDAY:

> He said unto them, An enemy hath done this. The servants said unto him, Wilt thou then that we go and gather them up?
>
> Matthew 13:28 (KJV)

Too often when you are shown the tares of your life, your answer to others, as well as yourself, is, the enemy did this! Should you then pick your life apart and "gather them up"? In that respect, yes! Remove the sin and tares from your life. You can then have a more intimate relationship with Christ. This verse goes deeper in thought and lesson. The tares in this parable are the unsaved among us. Some believe we are to live so separated that we have no contact with someone that is not of like faith or a Christian. Do you gather them up? For today, gather up the tares in your life and ask God what to do with them.

FRIDAY:

> But he said, Nay; lest while ye gather up the tares ye root up also the wheat with them.
>
> Matthew 13:29 (KJV)

I hope you kept Thursday on your mind and heart because here is God's answer: *no,* do not gather the unsaved up. Sometime you may tend to micro examine others and in doing so root them up, thinking they must be a tare. Are they? Is it your responsibility to root them up? Fruit inspector, are you? Does the inspector root up? How about an extra prayer for those you consider to be a tare? It could be that you are not such a skilled inspector. Be careful to not root up the good seed. Look to God to be the inspector and ask him to help you pray for the tare.

SATURDAY:

> Let both grow together until the harvest; and in the time of harvest I will say to the reapers, Gather ye together first the tares, and bind them in bundles to burn them: but gather the wheat into my barn.
>
> Matthew 13:30 (KJV)

A harvest is the crop that is gathered (ripe) in the season. God says to let the tares and the good seed grow together because a harvest or gathering will be done. *He* is the one that decides. The tares are gathered first. They will be bound together in bundles to burn.

Two thoughts as we close the week:

If you are being given notice that the tares are to be gathered together in bundles to burn, is that not even more incentive to begin anew and pray that they come to know Christ?

Remember the kingdom of heaven from Sunday? The verse used in Saturday's devotion ends telling us the wheat will be gathered and placed in *my barn.* Jesus had a simple manger for His first bed. His explanation in this parable for the kingdom of heaven is *his barn!* I don't know about you but I look forward to living in *his barn.* Will you be there?

Our Mansion

> Let not your heart be troubled; ye believe in God, believe also in me. In my Father's house are many mansions: if it were not so, I would have told you. I go to prepare a place for you. And if I go and prepare a place for you, I will come again, and receive you unto myself; that where I am, there ye may be also. And whither I go ye know, and the way ye know.
>
> John 14:1–4 (KJV)

Across our world, the size and style of homes range from "shanties," to "estates," to "mansions." While I drove to my home the other day, I felt a twinge of envy, as some homes were very elaborate, including the landscaping. My home is in the "remodel state." The Holy Spirit reminded me I will be united with Christ in heaven, and His children will *all* have mansions. We will all live in true equal housing.

John 14:1–4 above tells us our mansions are already there—no additional construction! Jesus is preparing a place for us. I assure you, His preparations leave nothing to be desired. As you read and pray over the thoughts for each day, may I challenge you to look around as you drive to and fro? Let the Holy Spirit speak to you with the homes you see—then as He speaks, let His wonderful love fill your soul.

SUNDAY:

> We have a building of God, an house not made with hands, eternal in the heavens.
>
> 2 Corinthians 5:1b (KJV)

If you have ever remodeled or built a house, then you know the perils of construction. It is one mess after the other. Stress builds, and we become troubled within. This stress leads us to emotional anguish. The pains can be so intense, we could be convinced our hearts were about to explode. The same can be said for your personal, emotional, and spiritual life. But we do not have to cater to that anguish. Our scripture verses begin with, "Let not your heart be troubled." Our hearts can be calm. Believe in Jesus Christ. Trust Him with your every care. Pray to Him. He will calm your troubled heart. Look for construction sites, as you are out today. When you gaze upon the "site," know this: Your mansion is already complete. Reflect on these thoughts below, allowing God to complete your personal, emotional, and spiritual mansion.

MONDAY:

> But my God shall supply all your need according to his riches in glory by Christ Jesus.
>
> Philippians 4:19 (KJV)

Living on your own, you are responsible for everything, such as: utilities, taxes, upkeep, food, and insurance. When you lived at home with your parents, they paid the bills, and you had need of nothing. God, your Father in heaven, is waiting to care for you, just like that. Look to Him in whatever need you have. The stresses of life, financial issues, a problem child or two, and relationships can be given over to our Father. Enjoy being under His care, and bask in His love for you. Today, see how many homes you can find having the appearance of an expert's care. Your Father leaves nothing unkept for us. Of that, we can be sure! What need(s) do you have that you can entrust in your Fathers care today?

TUESDAY:

I will never leave thee …

Hebrews 13:5 (KJV)

I saw a nice farmhouse up on a hill all alone. The barn was quite a distance from the house—no garage or carport—just the house. I thought to myself, *Wow, wouldn't that be nice.* Then I wondered, *Do the ones that live there ever get lonely?* When you go through a time of loneliness, it seems all too easy to let negativity and pain fester. However, when loneliness is gone, you actually see pressing forward to the love of God was what healed your heart. In heaven you will all be absorbed in praising Christ; here on earth you will not be lonely when you allow God to fill your heart with love.

WEDNESDAY:

Jesus saith unto him, I am the way, the truth, and the life:

John 14:6 (KJV)

Absolute honesty is the only way. Shades of the truth are not the truth; they are shades of a lie! The Word of God tells us Jesus is truth. If you are to be like Him, you should live the absolute truth. When you accept Jesus through salvation the Holy Spirit moves in, you are his temporary home. Allow the Holy Spirit to speak to your heart as you go through each day. Live the truth, breathe the truth, and sleep the truth. As you pass homes today, pray and ask the Holy Spirit to help you keep his home truthful.

THURSDAY:

> And I give unto them eternal life; and they shall never perish; neither shall any man pluck them out of my hand.
>
> John 10:28 (KJV)

A homestead is the owner's fixed residence and, in some states, is exempt from seizure and forced sale for the recovery of debts. Your home in heaven has been declared a homestead as well. The Lamb of God was slain and prepared your homestead, so you might enter into heaven, pure and wearing a robe of white as you meet your Father. Jesus' hand is secure. Once in his hand no one can remove you from your eternal home. Think of pulling into your driveway. Isn't it great to be home! Enjoy the thoughts of your eternal home each time you pull into the driveway of your earthly one. In the lines below list praises to Jesus for keeping your eternal home secure.

FRIDAY:

Even so, come, Lord Jesus.

Revelation 22:20b (KJV)

Do you enjoy having guests over? I love having family or friends come over to my home. It's fun to decorate or have a loved one over, after you have freshly cleaned or remodeled. Jesus tells us he will come again. Think about Jesus' return as you close your door after each visitor, and know that Jesus will return. Praise Ye the Lord! Are there things that need to be addressed before his return? Is your "home" cleaned and ready for Jesus' return?

SATURDAY:

And the Lord shall guide thee continually.

Isaiah 58:11a (KJV)

GPS: God's Positioning System. In today's world, we use a GPS to guide us from one point to another on the roadways. A voice will navigate instructions leading the way. If we make an incorrect turn, GPS corrects the path and points us to the corrected way. The verse in today's devotion tells us that the Lord will direct our way. God's Word is our GPS for His way. Sometimes life's temptations get you off course. With God as your pilot, there are no wrong turns. Carry your new GPS everywhere! As His Word tells us, "hide it in your heart." Have you missed a few turns recently? Make a list of destinations and let your new GPS plot the course.

Righteous

A very popular word used today is *righteous.* Youth and young twenties use it to express something that is good or above their expectations. When I looked righteous up in my thesaurus, I found words like: *godly, upright, just, moral, good,* and *puritanical.* Most of these words I understood right away, but I had to look further for puritanical. It can mean strict, severe, or rigid.

My topical Bible lists over thirty-four pages of verses having to do in some way with being and doing what is righteous. This week we are going to focus on the righteousness of Jesus and what that means to us.

SUNDAY:

> He made Him who knew no sin to be sin for us, that we might become the righteousness of God in Him.
>
> 2 Corinthians 5:21 (NKJV)

Besides the physical pain of the cross, Jesus bore the mental and emotional pain of sin. Not because He was sinful, but because He knew we were, are, and are going to be. Any pain we each feel is singular, meaning it is usually just for ourselves or sometimes just for some one person in particular. But Jesus felt the pain of any one who has lived or will live in the future. The pain He felt on the cross was upright, moral and good in the sense that He felt it strictly for you. He did it so you could "become the righteousness of God in Him."

Thank Him once again for your being able to be righteous in God.

MONDAY:

> Of Him you are in Christ Jesus, who became for us wisdom from God—and righteousness and sanctification and redemption.
>
> 1 Corinthians 1:30 (NKJV)

We often think of and thank Jesus for being our redemptor and Savior. But He is also our righteousness and our sanctification. Only through Him can we come to God with wisdom, righteousness, and sanctification. You must rely on Jesus in all you do and say. That is the only way you can become pure, upright and well advised.

Ask Him today to be your wisdom and make all you do or say righteous before God.

TUESDAY :

> Found in Him, not having my own righteousness, which is from the law, but that which is through faith in Christ, the righteousness which is from God by faith.
>
> Philippians 3:9 (NKJV)

Try as hard as we might, we can never do or say enough right things to become righteous. We are who we are, and we cannot follow all the rules all the time. It just will not happen. Not to worry! Through faith in Jesus Christ, we already have all the righteousness we need. But you must grow your faith in Christ. Growing faith is a daily, hour by hour process. You will not understand all the faith you get the day you accept Jesus as your redeemer. Understanding your faith and all it means to you will take persaverence and time. Praise the Father and the Son today for the righteousness freely given by faith.

WEDNESDAY:

> To him who does not work but believes on Him who justifies the ungodly, his faith is accounted for righteousness.
>
> Romans 4:5 (NKJV)

If our faith accounts for our righteousness, maybe we should be building that faith on a daily basis. There are those who will tell you faith only grows by trial. While faith can grow by trial, it is not the only way faith grows. Our faith can grow by spending time with God in prayer, reading His Word, and by joining together with other believers. I pray fervently you will spend more time in each of these endeavors this week. Faith can grow by assisting those less fortunate. Should you see someone with a need, step out and offer your aid. Sometimes even a little help can bring someone back to a hopeful state for their life.

Today, write about a time you helped someone outside your sphere of friends and family. Then remind yourself how it made a change in them and how you felt to see them on a new path.

THURSDAY:

> What the law could not do in that it was weak through the flesh, God did by sending His own Son in the likeness of sinful flesh, on account of sin.
>
> Romans 8:3 (NKJV)

God was so good to give the Israelites His laws. He was showing them He knew whom they were and how they were going to react. He understood flesh is weak. We have a Savior who is stronger than both the law and our weak flesh. He wants to tell you today: Don't count on yourself. Count on Me! Praise and Glory go to Jesus Christ and our Father who sent Him.

Write some of things you have been counting on through "the laws," and then tell yourself how it is so much better to have Jesus instead of your weak flesh.

FRIDAY:

> The work of righteousness will be peace; and the effect of righteousness, quietness and assurance forever.
>
> Isaiah 32:17 (NKJV)

This world and most days are filled with commotion, loud sounds, and lots of confusion. But because we have righteousness through Jesus Christ, we can call on Him anytime, anywhere, to fill our surroundings with quiet and confidence. He will give you peace when things are disruptive and nonsensical. Take your work today and give it over to Him, by asking Him to direct your every thought.

Ask Him to fill your life today with His peace, understanding, and righteousness.

SATURDAY:

> With the heart one believes unto righteousness, and with the mouth confession is made unto salvation.
>
> Romans 10:10 (NKJV)

From our mind comes reasoning. From our heart comes belief. With our eyes, we see God's wonders. With our ears, we hear His directions. With our mouths, we confess who He is to us and for us. Confess to others what He means to you in your life and theirs.

Today confess to Him how you might have sinned by not telling others who He is to you. Then tell Him how you will respond next time.

May Flower

"April showers bring May flowers, so what do May flowers bring? Pilgrims!" The Pilgrim leaders set sail for North America because they were concerned with losing their cultural identity. These men arranged with British investors to establish a new colony in North America. They faced a multitude of challenges. As Christians, we have good reason to be concerned with losing our cultural identity. Consider this question as you go through your daily devotions: Is my identity being shaped by today's culture or a Christian culture?

SUNDAY:

> Study to show thyself approved
>
> 2 Timothy 2:15 (KJV)

Once out of school, I thought I would be finished with having to study. But as I grew into my adulthood, studying became a way of life. I wanted to learn more. God tells us to study His Word. In a world of self-pleasure, we can maintain our Christian identity, as well as leave a legacy, by knowing the Word of God. What identity will your legacy leave?

MONDAY:

> For if any be a hearer of the word, and not a doer, he is like unto a man beholding his natural face in a glass: For he beholdeth himself, and goeth his way, and straightway forgetteth what manner of man he was. But whoso looketh into the perfect law of liberty, and continueth therein, he being not a forgetful hearer, but a doer of the work, this man shall be blessed in his deed.
>
> James 1:23–25 (KJV)

The Pilgrims were concerned for their identity so much they set sail. To be concerned is to be involved. The word concern also references self-concern. If you are not a doer of the Word, you may be self-concerned. Set sail today, and be a hearer and a doer. In what ways can you show concern for others?

TUESDAY:

> Either what woman having ten pieces of silver, if she lose one piece, doth not light a candle, and sweep the house, and seek diligently till she find it? And when she hath found it, she calleth her friends and her neighbours together, saying, "Rejoice with me; for I have found the piece, which I had lost." Likewise, I say unto you, there is joy in the presence of the angels of God over one sinner that repenteth.
>
> Luke 15:8–10 (KJV)

What would cause you to set sail and seek diligently? The pilgrims left their homeland to conserve their identity. They were concerned they were losing who they were and what they stood for in their homeland. In the verse today, the woman was so concerned over what she actually lost that she lit a candle and swept the house to search for it. Are you willing to seek diligently? Are you willing to give up a few of your personal pleasures to find your right relationship with Christ?

WEDNESDAY:

> Either what woman having ten pieces of silver, if she lose one piece, doth not light a candle, and sweep the house, and seek diligently till she find it?
>
> Luke 15:8 (KJV)

I remember being a young girl and trying to sweep up sugar I had spilled. Needless to say, it was very time consuming. I had to go over the area several times, and even then, I was not convinced I got all the grains. So then, I used a damp cloth to wipe the area. Sweeping your spiritual house can be like my sugar experience. Your life is ever changing and getting all the grains together may take some time, may even take a damp cloth. Get alone with God today, ask Him to help you sweep your house, so you may find that which was lost.

THURSDAY:

> And they awake him, and say unto him, "Master, carest thou not that we perish?"And he arose, and rebuked the wind, and said unto the sea, "Peace, be still." And the wind ceased, and there was a great calm. And he said unto them, "Why are ye so fearful? How is it that ye have no faith?"
>
> Mark 4:38b–40 (KJV)

The pilgrims originally set their site for the mouth of the Hudson River (modern day New York), but they arrived at the tip of Cape Cod, Massachusetts. There are times you arrive at a location other than where you planned. Like the ship's course, your course can be altered by storms. Stay with the faith God gives, and allow Him to still the storm and guide you to a safe landing. List below various alternate locations you have landed. How did this affect your plans and your life?

FRIDAY:

> And the LORD said unto Satan, Behold, all that he hath is in thy power; only upon himself put not forth thine hand. So Satan went forth from the presence of the LORD.
>
> Job 1:12 (KJV)

The *Mayflower* began its voyage with one hundred and two pilgrims, plus crew, and ended with fifty-three, including the crew. Challenges and death were real on their journey. They were real to Job and his family, too, but he stood fast. There are forty-two chapters in the book of Job. Struggle after struggle, Job continued to face challenges. The strength and faith he had in God carried him through. When you turn your back on a challenge, the challenge does not go away. You just don't see it. Trust in God with each challenge. He will give you the strength for your journey. Satan may be the power of this world but he only has power until God steps into the scene. What trial(s) are you facing?

SATURDAY:

> The LORD thy God in the midst of thee is mighty; he will save, he will rejoice over thee with joy; he will rest in his love, he will joy over thee with singing.
>
> Zephaniah 3:17 (KJV)

The Pilgrims completed their voyage and disembarked the ship to begin their new lives. With the LORD, you, too, can disembark, and begin your new life. Keep God as your focal point, for He is mighty. Rest in His love today, and keep your Christian cultural identity alive. He "will joy over thee with singing!" What ways can you keep your beliefs alive?

Father's Day

We put a day on our calendars to remind us to celebrate our earthly fathers. We honor them for the love they gave us, for being there for us when we have hurts of any kind and picking up the pieces. Those times when they stopped us from doing the things we really wanted to do but knew we should not. We don't have a calendar to remind us to honor our heavenly father. It is unfortunate that we need to be reminded to celebrate what He has done and continues to do for us. Our reminder is the devotions this week, as you go through this week, mark your calendar to enjoy every day of your life as a child of God.

SUNDAY:

> For God so loved the world that He gave His one and only Son, that whoever believes in him shall not perish but have eternal life.
>
> John 3:16 (NIV)

Our Father gave His only Son so you could be adopted into His family. Jesus died on the cross for your sins. When you accept Jesus as your Savior and ask His forgiveness, you are given eternal life in His kingdom.

Today rejoice with God for your adoption into His family and write about it below.

MONDAY:

Have we not all one Father? Did not one God create us?

Malachi 2:10a (NIV)

God is your Father and Creator. He is your origin and your beginning. Your earthly father may have helped you to come into this world, but your Father in heaven was your architect. Enjoy the child He made of you.

Speak to God in your writing below on how you are enjoying being His child.

TUESDAY:

> "If we are thrown into the blazing furnace, the God we serve is able to save us from it, and he will rescue us from your hand, O King."
>
> Daniel 3:17 (NIV)

He is able to save you from the "blazing furnace," which you can be thrown into, or walk into on your own. Not only is He able to save you, but He will save you. He saved Shadrach, Meshach, and Abednego from the fiery furnace. He will save you from the fiery furnace, in your every day life, and from the fires of hell. All you have to do is ask. He will.

Use the lines below to ask God to save you from the fires of hell. If He has already saved you from those fires, use the lines to thank Him.

WEDNESDAY:

> In you our fathers put their trust; they trusted and you delivered them.
>
> Psalm 22:4 (NIV)

No matter what, you can trust in the one true God. You may not have completely trusted your earthly father, or you may have trusted him totally to rescue you from your trials. Whichever was true of your earthly father, your heavenly Father is trustworthy. Trust in Him to deliver you from any and every difficult situation you encounter. He is with you during those testing times.

Use the space below to inform Him of the trials He has rescued you from and then praise Him.

THURSDAY:

> Consequently, faith comes from hearing the message, and the message is heard through the word of Christ.
>
> Romans 10:17 (NIV)

How do you hear Him? You hear Him by being in His Word, by having faith in Him, and by witnessing what He has done for you. Through these daily devotions, you are taking part in hearing what He says to you. Listen for His still, small voice. He will have something wonderful to say.

Write below what you hear Him telling you today.

FRIDAY:

Your righteousness is everlasting and your law is true.

Psalm 119:142 (NIV)

His righteousness and truth are everlasting. The laws He gave Moses are as true today as they were when Moses received them. If you ask Him to be your Savior, He is everlastingly and ever present with you. He will abide in you until you meet Him in heaven. You will not be without Him.

Honor Him for His presence in you and your life with the lines below.

SATURDAY

> Then I heard what sounded like a great multitude, like the roar of rushing waters and like loud peals of thunder, shouting: Hallelujah! For our God Reigns.
>
> Revelation 19:6 (NIV)

This verse reminds me of the sound of thunder from a recent storm. The feeling of the "thunder" seemed to be in my backyard. The loudness was crying out "Our God Reigns;" it thrilled my heart and magnified my soul. The next time you hear thunder, shout from your soul, "Our God Reigns."

Maybe it isn't raining and thundering today, but remember a time it was and use the area below to shout from your soul how God reigns.

PART II

summer

Let an all-powerful God refresh your hot dry Spirit!

SUMMER

Daughter, sister, mother, wife,
And now there's a salaried
Position in my life.

Each day I run to and fro,
Sustaining Me has met a new low.

I ponder the words,
"He has Risen" and know for me,
All He has given.

Daily I search
Throughout His teachings
For His answers to my beseeching.

All my hats I wear at one time,
Because it is His cross
I bear and not mine.

—Kathleen J. Jones—

Wearing many hats, we become hot and flustered. We begin to drown in our own sweat. Through summer's devotions, we find God's Word cools the hot dry spirit.

Elohim

This week, we are going to discuss "praying" a name of God. Elohim is pronounced e-lo-HEEM and means creator. Hopefully, we can create a habit of addressing God with one of His holy names. As you complete each of the daily devotions, try to use Elohim specifically in your prayer. Get to know your Father in a deeper way, as each day passes.

SUNDAY:

In the beginning God created the heavens and the earth.

Genesis 1:1 (NKJV)

This verse is so short; we often just slip by it without thinking it through. In ten short words we are told there is nothing we see, touch, smell, or hear and the air we breathe that He did not create. Take the day, and notice everything around you, everything you use in your day, and everything your mind conceives. Then thank Elohim for it all.

MONDAY:

Then God said let there be light; and there was light.

Genesis 1:3 (NKJV)

Ever been in a terrible storm late at night and all the electricity went out? This storm took all the lights in your entire area. What did it feel like? It happened to me, and I was scarred to death. I couldn't see well enough to find the candles. I was alone, it was dark, and there was no moon or stars, just dark and wind and rain. Praise Elohim today for *all* the light He provides in those dark times and every day.

TUESDAY:

> Then God said, "Let Us make man in Our image, according to Our likeness.
>
> Genesis 1:26 (NKJV)

God loves you so much; even from the beginning, He wanted you in His image and according to the likeness of Jesus, the Holy Spirit, and all His angels. He has so much confidence in you; He never questioned making you in His image. He just made His decision, loved you, and "made His desire." We, then, become accountable for the choices we make in our life. God does not force us to "live" in His image and likeness. He made us so we make our own choices in this life. Confess to Elohim today your responsibility for being made in His image and likeness. Lift praises to Him for His loving you so much.

WEDNESDAY:

> So God created man in His own image; in the image of God He created him; male and female He created them.
>
> Genesis 1:27 (NKJV)

I was once told if God said something more than once, it must be important. Two verses next to one another state the same thought. I hope you have considered what being in God's image means to you. If you have not considered that, then do it today. If you have considered being in God's image, then ask yourself and Elohim if there are any changes you need to make in your daily living, so others can see you in His image.

THURSDAY:

Then God blessed them.

Genesis 1:28a (NKJV)

So let me get this straight: God did all the work, and then He blessed man and woman. This picture is so backwards to our world today. Most everyone wants a pat on the back before they have finished the job, and they definitely want all the blessing for any work they may or may not have done. Maybe, I'm wrong on that thought! But I'm not wrong in that God has not changed. He blesses us for work He has done. Now that is your God of gods.

FRIDAY:

> Fill the earth and subdue it; have dominion over the fish of the sea, over the birds of the air, and over every living thing that moves on the earth.
>
> Genesis 1:28b (NKJV)

Okay, so not only does He bless man and woman, but He gives us dominion (authority) over all He has created. When is the last time you know of someone who created something from nothing and then handed control over to someone else? Let me think—never. Now that is confidence in One's creation! It is also evidence of His love. Lift up your voice today to Elohim for His confidence in you and all His creations. Take a moment to sing His praises using His name Elohim.

List what you might be able to take better care of for Him.

SATURDAY:

> Then God blessed the seventh day and sanctified it, because in it He rested from all his work which God had created and made.
>
> Genesis 2:3 (NKJV)

As I have noted before, *to sanctify* is "to make holy." God made the seventh day holy, and He rested from all His work. We, as Christians, use Sunday (the first day) to call holy and rest. The reason we do that is because Sunday is the day of the week Jesus rose from the grave. Actually, I believe each day God has made is holy. But the scripture tells us to use the day for holiness and rest. Do you rest on His holy day? If God did it, shouldn't you? I do understand we have so much to do in our human lives. So are we saying God did less in His holy life? Not a fair question? Or do you just not like the answer? Remember to rest tomorrow, and while you do, give Elohim one more day to hear from your heart how glorious He is.

His Refreshing Preparations

Life is filled with preparations we must make. Some preparations may take months, weeks or just days. If you are a mom, you prepare meals everyday. If you are a student, you prepare for final exams over a three-month time period. If you have a job outside the home, you prepare your bosses requests whenever he (she) asks you to. Our God is a God of preparations. He is preparing a place for you.

> Thou preparest a table before me in the presence of my enemies; Thou anoints my head with oil; My cup runs over."
>
> Psalm 23:5 (NKJV)

SUNDAY:

> Thou preparest a table before me in the presence of my enemies; Thou anoints my head with oil; My cup runs over."
>
> Psalm 23:5 (NKJV)

Thou preparest

An invitation has arrived for dinner with friends. Of course you accept: no cooking, no cleaning, and no menu you have to think up. Plus, they are your friends. But when you arrive, five minutes prior to the invitations noted time, you notice there is no aroma coming from the kitchen. The table isn't set, and the hosts aren't even finished dressing. Verse five promises "God prepares." He sets a date, a time, a place, and sends you an invitation. When you step to His door, the menu has been set and food assembled and cooked. The presentation is elegant and everything is at the correct serving temperature. All you have to do is sit down, and enjoy what He has prepared.

Remind yourself below how you might have felt when you showed up and prepartions had not been made.

MONDAY:

> Thou preparest a table before me in the presence of my enemies; Thou anoints my head with oil; My cup runs over."
>
> Psalm 23:5 (NKJV)

a table before me

When you arrived, your friend's dinner table was stacked with books, toys, and weekly papers. Before you could sit down, you, not only had to clear the mess, ready the table with eating utensils, but you also had to find a chair. God's table has the most elegant cloth you can imagine—with matching napkins. You instantly notice each place setting is of the finest china and stemware. Eating utensils are, of course, gold. Serving dishes are all of crystal. The chair He offers reminds you of a throne. It is clear His table is complete.

Tell God below your first impressions of the table He has set before you.

TUESDAY:

> Thou preparest a table before me in the presence of my enemies; Thou anoints my head with oil; My cup runs over."
>
> Psalm 23:5 (NKJV)

in the presence of my enemies;

God has not only planned and prepared for you, He has also placed you on a throne. In addition, He does all of this for all to see. Our verse says "in the presence of my enemies." An enemy can be a rival, someone who has caused you pain, or someone who just makes you feel uncomfortable. The Lord wants everyone to know how much He loves you and wants to provide for you. He wants even our worst foes to be told in the boldest of ways how important you are as His child.

Below tell your Lord thank you for placing you at the forefront of your foes.

WEDNESDAY:

> Thou preparest a table before me in the presence of my enemies; Thou anoints my head with oil; My cup runs over."
>
> Psalm 23:5 (NKJV)

Thou anoint my head

In biblical times, only leaders, the very important, and/or rich were anointed. The anointing had very important and significant reasoning. David was anointed by Samuel, the priest of priests, in the presence of His father and brothers. First Samuel 16:13a tells us the Spirit of the Lord came upon David from that day forward.

This verse tells us God anoints our head. We are anointed by the one true God, our Lord, Master, and Savior. We are that important to Him. All we have to do is let Him do the anointing. Even though He is your Lord and Master, you are to hold your head high. Walk, talk, and think with His warmth and tenderness.

Why do you think God would anoint your head rather than some other body part? (There is no wrong answer; it is your thoughts.)

THURSDAY:

> Thou preparest a table before me in the presence of my enemies; Thou anoints my head with oil; My cup runs over."
>
> Psalm 23:5 (NKJV)

with oil;

Then and now, oil is very precious and costly. These fragrant oils were prepared according to a recipe given by God at the time the Israelites left Egypt, making them rare and considered holy.

Today, we use fragrant oils to sooth our skin in winter and to soothe our temperaments. We use specific oils to heal burns and cuts. Take all of these properties, and know God has additives we haven't even considered. He offers healings we cannot understand. He fills our senses with fragrances we have never experienced. His oil is the oil of everlasting salvation. We only have to offer our head for His anointing oil.

Think and write today how this aromatic warm oil poured lightly on your head will affect your senses and your state of well being.

FRIDAY:

> Thou preparest a table before me in the presence of my enemies; Thou anoints my head with oil; My cup runs over."
>
> Psalm 23:5 (NKJV)

My cup

Almost everyone has a favorite cup or glass from which they prefer to drink their favorite beverage. As time elapses, you have to refill the cup each time you want to enjoy your beverage. It is a manual, continuous process. You fill it; it fills you. Consider the beverage is a need, a hurt, an illness, a loved one for whom you are concerned. You are the cup. You are filled with this beverage. But aren't we sometime really feeling empty? There just isn't anymore of you to give or do. Ask God to fill your cup with His beverage, and it will be filled. You are God's cup, so let Him decide what to fill you with today.

What beverage do you need to fill your cup today? Ask Him below to fill you by His grace.

SATURDAY:

> Thou preparest a table before me in the presence of my enemies; Thou anoints my head with oil; My cup runs over."
>
> Psalm 23:5 (NKJV)

runs over.

Ever been out to eat and the server only filled your cup half full? Or the server poured your first cup full but never came back to ask if you needed more? Did it make you want to ask, "Hey, are you running out of coffee back there?"

When God is your server, your cup is never half full. Our scripture tells us God supplies our needs to overflowing. He remains at our table to fill your cup continually. Call upon the Lord to be your server, and allow Him to fill you with His goodness and mercy the rest of your days.

Tell God how thankful you are today He is your server.

Songs

Worshiping the Lord comes in many forms. One of the ways is in song. We have favorite songs or lyrics that really bring us into a worship mode. In those times of dryness, singing can bring calmness and refresh you. This week, we are going to take different verses in the Bible where song is mentioned or God's people rose up in song to worship. As you go through this week, keep a song in your heart for God. You can worship Him with His words. It does not have to be a song you hear on the radio. Just take His words, and sing them back to Him.

SUNDAY:

> Sing O Daughter of Zion; shout aloud, O Israel! Be glad and rejoice with all your heart.
>
> Zephaniah 3:14 (NIV)

This scripture says it all! Sing aloud to God today. Shout to him, and be glad, for He has set you free. Rejoice in Him today with all your heart. There is no other that "can do" or "will do" what He has done and will do for you. So Sing!

Use the lines below to write your song to the Lord. Tell Him of all the wonderous things He has done for you.

MONDAY:

Sing and make music in your heart to the Lord.

Ephesians 5:19 (NIV)

Continue to praise Him in song today. Bring the music from your heart to allow your praise to come from within. The music will be beautiful sounds to your Father in heaven. All around you will enjoy the sound, as they hear Him being praised.

Allow the words from your heart to ring out to the Lord in the space below.

TUESDAY:

I will sing with my spirit, but I will also sing with my mind.

1 Corinthians 14:15 (NIV)

So far this week, you shouted to The Lord and sung with your heart. Now sing with your mind and your spirit. Allow any anger or annoyance you may have in your mind to be set free. Give it all to Him. Let there be nothing left of you that is not praising Him today.

Speak to Him of the anger you are holding in your heart, write it out and allow Him to take it from you.

WEDNESDAY:

I will sing for the one I love.

Isaiah 5:1 (NIV)

Songs of love are numerous, some will speak of the love you have lost, or the love you have for the man or woman in this world. There are even songs of love for the Lord. Today, sing only of love to your Father. No other can love you the way He does, give the love back to Him in song. Show Him how much you love Him by singing just to Him.

Let Him know how much you love Him in writing a love song to Him today.

THURSDAY:

Sing to him a new song.

Psalm 33:3 (NIV)

Take anything you have today that will make music. It may be a pencil you tap on your leg. It makes music when you are praising Your Lord. Sing to Him with words you feel, words you think about Him. It is a new song to Him. Let Him hear your music.

Use that pencil you were tapping with to write out those words below.

FRIDAY:

> Hear this, you kings! Listen, you rulers! I will sing to the Lord, I will sing; I will make music to the Lord, the God of Israel.
>
> Judges 5:3 (NIV)

This verse is a song. It is the beginning of the "Song of Deborah" when God gave the Israelites victory. Sing with Deborah as she sang praises to God for the victory she was given. Remember the victories you have been given by God. Let the rulers and the kings of the times you were chained, hear you praising the One who set you free and gave you victory.

What are the victories you have been given, write them below.

SATURDAY:

> Then I heard every creature in heaven and on earth and under the earth and the sea and all that is in them, singing;
>
> Revelation 5:13 (NIV)

All the creatures are singing, "Worthy is the Lamb." Close this week in song, telling Him and all you know; He is worthy. He was slain for you. Praise Him for all He has done. As Deborah sang, you also sing for the victory He has given you. Raise your hands as you sing, "You Are Worthy! Worthy is the Lamb!"

Write your praises out. Writing helps in the praising.

What Waiting Can Bring

Ever heard the old saying, "Good things come to those who wait?" Waiting for anything is not my gift. I get anxious, walk the floor, and generally just stay irritable. But waiting on God's plan and timing is important to our well being. This week, let's talk about what waiting can mean in the long run.

SUNDAY:

> And being assembled together with them, He commanded them not to depart from Jerusalem, but to wait for the Promise of the Father, "which," He said, "You have heard from me;"
>
> Acts 1:4 (NKJV)

Jesus was with His disciples just before He ascended to His Father in heaven. Before leaving, He did two things: he instructed them to *wait* and reminded them of a *promise* given. Waiting is always hard, especially if what we wait for is significant. The disciples were waiting for the largest gift ever to be given. The only gift any bigger was Jesus' death on the cross. Jesus told them previously of this promise, but it was so important, He mentioned it again. If Christ has asked you to wait at any time, the outcome must be huge. So wait with His patience, His love, and His expectations.

Tell God below what you are waiting on today.

MONDAY:

> For John truly baptized with water, but you shall be baptized with the Holy Spirit not many days from now.
>
> Acts 1:5 (NKJV)

To be baptized is to be immersed. John immersed with water. But now, not only has Christ promised the Holy Spirit, but also He promised the disciples would be immersed with the Holy Spirit. This same promise belongs to each of us. When we accept Jesus as our personal Savior, we are immersed with the Holy Spirit. This means the Holy Spirit covers us from head to toe, inside and out. He covers our thoughts, what we see, hear, and breathe. He covers our bodies, so everything we touch is also touched by the Holy Spirit. These are the reasons we are to stay holy. We should not be responsible for putting the Holy Spirit in or on anything, which can be deemed unholy. Remember your immersion today.

Who might you touch today that you could be touching with the Holy Spirit? Write to yourself now how you might touch them and what you might say.

TUESDAY:

> Therefore, when they had come together, they asked Him, saying, "Lord, will You at this time restore the kingdom to Israel?"
>
> Acts 1:6 (NKJV)

When I read today's verses, the question that comes immediately to mind is, "Did you hear what He is giving you?" As soon as I ask, I am reminded of the times I have been waiting so very long, and my mind goes back to things I wanted in the past; and yet they still have not come to fruition. The disciples were also stuck on what they wanted from the past. But instead of being stuck in the past, we should stay on tract with what Jesus wants for us now. Remind yourself what He wants for you today and in the future.

WEDNESDAY:

> And He said to them, "It is not for you to know times or seasons which the Father has put in His own authority."
>
> Acts 1:7 (NKJV)

I feel like I hear a little frustration in Jesus when He speaks the above passage. But it is just my interpretation. Scripture tells us He is patient beyond our comprehension. Frustrated or not, Jesus was emphatic: "It is not for you to know!" The word *surprise* indicates something that is unexpected, and yet it is our human nature to want to know ahead of schedule. But Jesus says, "Trust in me, in the Father." Know He has the perfect time and season for all things. Wait for His surprise today. He will follow through.

Thank Him today that He has the perfect timing for all our surprises, even those we do not understand at the time we receive them.

THURSDAY:

> And He said to them, "It is not for you to know times or seasons which the Father has put in His own authority."
>
> Acts 1:7 (NKJV)

Some of us, by nature, take all the authority others will let us have. Some of us want others to take the authority. For those who do not care to be authoritative, following this scripture is a little easier. For those of us who want all authority, this scripture should be memorized and repeated daily. It is God Himself who has put authority under His power. This is authority over all things, including when to answer prayers immediately, later, or perhaps not in the way we expect. Life has taught me, I do not have the experience to know what is best and when is best. God, in His infinite wisdom and love, knows and delivers when the time is exactly right for all concerned. Remember this day answers affect all those around us, and God looks out for all.

Write some things you may have asked for and wanted immediately, but now that you look backwards the answer then would have been exactly the wrong.

FRIDAY:

> But you shall receive power when the Holy Spirit has come upon you;
>
> Acts 1: 8a (NKJV)

Take a moment, and think about something you prayed for; but you had to wait to receive. When God answered, did it not leave you with a powerful feeling? The Holy Spirit is powerful. By Him and through Him, we can accomplish anything. God's Word promises that. We often do not call upon this power, but that does not mean it is not there. This power is not to be used foolishly or selfishly, but you are called to use it. Today use the power of the Holy Spirit to witness in a new way to someone you love or just someone you know.

Remind yourself what you might have prayed at one time, and when it was answered made you feel all powerful.

SATURDAY:

> And you shall be witnesses to Me in Jerusalem, and in all Judea and Samaria, and to the end of the earth.
>
> Acts 1:8b (NKJV)

This is the day we have waited for, the day of our witness for Him. Matter-of-fact, this is the day He has waited for, the day you would call upon Him to become the witness He deserves. We have all waited long enough. Pull out all the stops! Call upon the Holy Spirit you have been immersed in, and witness in your work place, your city, your state, and throughout the world.

Take a moment and write out your witness for Him that you can use daily.

Church of Philadelphia

How much do you use your Bible? Do you find yourself looking for it when it is time to go to church? Is dust collecting? The church of Philadelphia utilized God's Word. As you go through the devotionals for this week consider how you can make the most of the Word of God. You will find ways to dispell the old man and develop your new life with a calm and poised spirit.

SUNDAY:

> And to the angel of the church in Philadelphia write; These things saith he that is holy, he that is true, he that hath the key of David, he that openeth, and no man shutteth; and shutteth, and no man openeth;
>
> Revelation 3:7 (KJV)

To think that our God will set an open door before us that no man can shut is amazing. Being a loser of keys, I have been locked out a time or two. Trying to find a way inside is exasperating. God will give you an open door to be a witness for Him. In the United States of America, we have an open door to follow Him. Do you follow Him? You can say a lot with your mouth, but what are you saying with your actions? Watch for the open doors He gives you?

MONDAY:

> I know thy works: behold, I have set before thee an open door, and no man can shut it: for thou hast a little strength.
>
> Revelation 3:8 (KJV)

How strong are you? God's Word tells us we are fighting a spiritual battle. Our strength is little. We are made strong through Christ. Rely on His strength to make you strong. In what ways can you be strengthened? Make a list of your strengths and weaknesses, then practice using both.

TUESDAY:

And hast kept my word.

Revelation 3:8 (KJV)

Can you imagine meeting God face to face and hearing Him say to you, "You kept my Word?" The church of Philadelphia is definitely special. How were they able to hear these words from God? You may say to yourself, "I can not keep all His Word. I am not perfect. Even God tells us we are not perfect." You are right; we are not perfect, which is why we cannot keep His entire Word. However, when we repent, we keep His Word. You see, part of His Word also tells us to repent. How can you keep His Word, unless you know it? Make a renewed commitment today to learn God's Word and keep it.

WEDNESDAY:

And hast not denied my name.

Revelation 3:8 (KJV)

Deny—what a word! Have you ever been in denial when things around you are not what you would like them to be, or maybe you are not what you want to be? Whatever the situation, being in denial is not accepting the truth. God is truth. This church did not deny his name. They accepted God and accepted Him for who *He* is. Do you accept God for all He is? Be like the church of Philadelphia: accept God, and do not deny His name.

THURSDAY:

> Because thou hast kept the word of my patience, I also will keep thee from the hour of temptation, which shall come upon all the world, to try them that dwell upon the earth.
>
> Revelation 3:10 (KJV)

Satan and his demons will come to you in hoards at times, fighting with everything they can, and in every way they can. God will not allow you to be tempted above that which you are able to bear. The choice is yours! God keeps the door open for you. What will your choice be when you are tempted? He can and will keep you from temptation. But you must ask. Do you ask? What temptations are you facing that you can ask God to help you bear?

FRIDAY:

> Behold, I come quickly: hold that fast which thou hast, that no man take thy crown.
>
> Revelation 3:11 (KJV)

Is there a consequence to not holding fast to God's Word? Yes, you can lose a reward. I am reminded of the first time my husband held our firstborn. Our child was so tiny, and my husband did not want to drop him. As I watched while he held our little boy, I noticed the baby's leg was a light shade of blue. His father was holding fast! That is the way we are to hold on to the things of God—with a strong tight grip. Are there some things slipping through your fingers? Maybe you need to tighten the grip and hold fast to God's Word. List those areas below and pray for strength to hold on tight.

SATURDAY:

> Him that overcometh will I make a pillar in the temple of my God, and he shall go no more out: and I will write upon him the name of my God, and the name of the city of my God, which is new Jerusalem, which cometh down out of heaven from my God: and I will write upon him my new name.
>
> Revelation 3:12 (KJV)

When you have times that the word *overcome* does not fit into your vocabulary, remember this verse. God says He will make you a pillar. Pillars are the *major* support in any building. You can overcome, and when you do, you are able to be a *major* support for others. What a joy to know you can actually be a helper to someone else! Oh, I know there are times you cannot even help yourself, let alone another, but isn't that what we are here for: to be able to be a support for each other when we can? To Him that overcometh, I will make a pillar! Decide how you can be a support for others. Use the space below to write some ideas down. Be an "overcomer."

Our Father

Life is made up of titles. Even when we don't agree with a particular title for a particular person, the title is still there for others to hear. Because we look to God to be our Lord, our Master, and our Savior we often forget to address Him as 'Our Father.'

SUNDAY:

A Father to the fatherless, and a defender of the widow, is God in His holy habitation."

Psalm 68:5 (NKJV)

If you had an earthly father who was very attentive to you growing up, it isn't hard to imagine or understand what it means to call our Lord, "Our Father." Words that describe this position in life consist of protector, provider, teacher, trainer, fixer, patient, strong, and decision maker, just to name a few. Take time today to think on these titles. Even if your earthly father did not meet these names, your heavenly Father does.

Thank Him today for the times He met some of these titles so far in your life.

MONDAY:

> But now, O' Lord, You are our Father; We are the clay, and You our potter; And all we are the work of Your Hand."
>
> Isaiah 64:8 (NKJV)

Ever feel like your life is spinning out of control? The only way to make clay into a perfect "pot" is to spin it on a wheel as it is being shaped. The best part of our life of clay is that Jesus Christ our Savior, Lord, and Father is the one pressing the feed for the spin. His hands shape our "pot." These are steady hands, never wavering, never pressing too tightly or lightly. His touch is always one of perfection.

Write today how His perfect touch has shaped you.

TUESDAY:

> Doubtless You are our Father, Though Abraham was ignorant of us, And Israel does not acknowledge us. You, O LORD, are our Father; Our Redeemer from Everlasting is Your name.
>
> Isaiah 63:16 (NKJV)

From the very beginning, to the everlasting of time, the "point" is: The Lord Jesus Christ is our Father, our Redeemer. Even those who came before us and had no knowledge of us or those within our midst today who refuse to admit we belong to the Lord, do not matter. The only true "point" is the Lord our Father. Isaiah says, it does not matter whom or when, no one can argue this "point." Remind yourself of this point several times today.

Is there someone in your past or even in you're here and now who is ignorant of who you are in Christ? Speak to your Father today; let Him put your mind at ease.

WEDNESDAY:

> For who ever does the will of My Father in heaven is my brother and sister and mother.
>
> Matthew 12:50 (NKJV)

Jesus calls the Lord, His Father. He tells us many times, if we obey or follow the wishes of His Father, we become His sister(s)/brother(s). This can only mean His Father becomes our Father. The only stipulation for this equation is that we must do the will of the Father. What is His will for you today? Today is all you need to think about. His will for you is so finely planned; you only have to follow one day at a time. Ask forgiveness where you failed yesterday. Follow Him today. Tomorrow has been settled by the Father.

Do not think about tomorrow, but discover what His will is for you today. Tell Him what you believe that will to be.

THURSDAY:

> And whenever you stand praying, if you have anything against anyone, forgive him, that your Father in heaven may also forgive you your trespasses.
>
> Mark 11:25 (NKJV)

We are told at least twice in God's Word we must forgive those that trespass against us. That is the only way God will forgive us. Scripture says "anything against anyone." Anything! Anyone! Pretty big area! But guess what? This also includes *you.* Yep, you must forgive you. So dig down today, and confess that torment you have been carrying as baggage. Confess it to yourself. Now that it is confessed, forgive yourself. It is over. Gone. *Finished.* You belong to the Father. He forgives you too.

Remind yourself today what He has forgiven you and what you have forgiven yourself also.

FRIDAY:

> No one can come to me unless the Father who sent me draws him; and I will raise him up at the last day.
>
> John 6:44 (NKJV)

Jesus states in order for us to get to Him, our Father must first have called us or drawn us to Him. So our Father not only forgives us but calls us. Do you have a memory of your earthly father calling you as a child? If you do not remember your earthly father, then do you remember someone else calling you?

This calling for you must have been important. Think it through. The person calling you had to stop what they were doing, walk to the porch or another room, decide words to use, adjust their voice to the appropriate level, so you could hear; and then the caller had to engage the brain to speak. Even though calling out is something we do every day, it is a process. Our heavenly Father is responsible for calling us to our Savior. It is a process. Try to understand the process God used for calling you to Him.

Think on that today. Then thank Him.

SATURDAY:

> Then Jesus answered and said to them "Most assuredly, I say to you, the Son can do nothing of Himself, but what He sees the Father do; for whatever He does, the Son also does in like manner."
>
> John 5:19 (NKJV)

Jesus knew what to do, only because He saw the Father do it. How is it we expect ourselves to do anything without seeing our Father do it? There is only one way we can "see our Father" do anything. We have to read His Word, contemplate His Word, pray His Word, and then do His Word. All our steps and happenings are in His Word. Our only responsibilities are to see, to watch, and to do in like manner.

Today, think on one action verb (telling who God is, reading in the synagogue, etc.) that you know Jesus performed. Read it, contemplate it, pray about it, and then do it.

You Are God's Specialty

We can all be known for running the gambit of emotions in a very short time span. God made us this way, and He has a plan for us to follow, no matter in which seat of the emotional roller coaster we sit. Even before Jesus was born a man God made provisions for us to be cooled by life's "heating up" happenings.

SUNDAY:

> So that the priests could not continue ministering because of the cloud; for the glory of the Lord filled the house of God.
>
> 2 Chronicles 5:14 (nkjv)

> Blessed are those who mourn, for they shall inherit the earth.
>
> Matthew 5:4 (nkjv)

Day one, you wake up feeling really good and upbeat. You know you have issues that must be dealt with, but it is "all good;" and God will supply. Then, you receive information that literally leaves you gasping for breath in your lungs and heart.

Think on a day this was true for you. Journal it today.

MONDAY:

> The Lord your God, who goes before you, He will fight for you according to all He did for you in Egypt before your eyes.
>
> Deuteronomy 1:30 (NKJV)

> For God is not the author of confusion but of peace, as in all the churches of the saints.
>
> 1 Corinthians 14:33 (NKJV)

Day two, you wake up in a daze. You try to reprocess yesterday's information, but you just cannot get any of it to make sense. You are totally confused for yourself and your loved ones. Then, you become protective toward those you love. Your mind races to what questions they will have. Can you answer their questions, and will they worry needlessly?

How did your loved ones react to the news you wrote about yesterday? Journal what your concerns were for them and yourself.

TUESDAY:

> For I know the thoughts that I think toward you, says the Lord, thoughts of peace and not of evil, to give you a future and a hope.
>
> Jeremiah 29:11 (NKJV)

> Therefore submit to God. Resist the devil and he will flee from you.
>
> James 4:7 (NKJV)

Day three, the moment your eyes open, the scriptures begin to flood your mind. They are reassuring scriptures, full of love and hope. Then, almost immediately, your mind becomes confused, because you cannot find any logical reasoning about your information. But we are told to resist the devil. We can only do that by submitting ourselves to Christ in any crisis. You can submit to Christ by remembering the scriptures and using them to yourself out loud and in your talks with God.

Find some scriptures today that you can hold in your mind for these situations. Journal them and go back to them often.

WEDNESDAY:

> He who is slow to anger is better than the mighty, and he who rules his spirit than he who takes a city.
>
> Proverbs 16:32 (NKJV)

> For God has not given us a spirit of fear, but of Power and of love and of a sound mind.
>
> 2 Timothy 1:7 (NKJV)

Day four, you spend most of the day replaying the last three days. You begin to feel angry. You are angry at yourself, angry at the information, and angry that even on the Internet, there are no explanations. Then, you call a friend and discuss the information and just how you feel. You confess you really do not know how you feel. You are so confused. All confidence in what you thought you knew is gone.

Both scriptures tell us this anger and confusion is not from God. Thank Him today He has given you power and love and a sound mind.

THURSDAY:

> Therefore do not cast away your confidence, which has great reward. For you have need of endurance, so that after you have done the will of God, you may receive the promise.
>
> Hebrews 10:35–36 (NKJV)

> There is therefore now no condemnation to those who are In Christ Jesus, who do not walk according to the flesh, But according to the Spirit."
>
> Romans 8:1 (NKJV)

Day five, some explanations for your information have suddenly come through. It all seems so simple. Why, you ask yourself, was the information not given in this manner in the beginning? Then, you audibly berate yourself by softly speaking, "Oh ye of little faith." Remind yourself often there is no condemnation to those who are in Christ. That means there is no need to feel anger at yourself or be confused by any one else. The answers are always with God.

Instead of berating yourself, journal your thanks to God who does not condemn but instead wants to lift your confidences and hand you a great reward.

FRIDAY:

> Let your conduct be without covetousness; be content with such things as you have, For He Himself has said, "I will never leave you nor forsake you."
>
> Hebrews 13:5 (NKJV)

> Beloved, now we are children of God; and it has not yet been revealed what we shall be, but we know that when He is revealed, we shall be like Him, for we shall see Him as He is.
>
> 1 John 3:2 (NKJV)

Day six, you awaken knowing there are issues to deal with, but God will supply.

Journal how you will react in the weeks to come now that your confedence in God, Jesus, and the Holy Spirit has changed.

SATURDAY:

I will bless the Lord at all times; His praise shall continually be in my mouth.

Psalm 34:1 (NKJV)

It is good to give thanks to the Lord, and to sing praises to Your name, O Most High.

Psalm 92:1 (NKJV)

The Lord is great and greatly to be praised; He is to be feared above all gods.

Psalm 96:4 (NKJV)

Day seven, your heart, mind, and soul are full of praises. You now have a day of rest, and you are welcoming your new ability to leave it all to Him in His time. Journal your praises to Him then say them out loud. I am told what we hear and write stays with us twice as long as just what we write.

Letting Go and Letting God

At times, I find myself in a pool of my very own "needing to let go" and wondering if I am going under for the last time. To illustrate my point, I recently saw a chipmunk caught in the middle of a backyard swimming pool. How long had he been in there? With the strength he had left, he paddled his feet as fast as he could, struggling with all his might to stay afloat. As I stood and watched out for him, my friend ran to get the pool net. I could see him fighting for what seemed to be his last breath. Several jerks of his head told me in no uncertain terms we had to help and quick. With one scoop of the net, he was safe. His breathing was faint, and we could tell he was so tired. He lay there for some time. Then after gaining just enough strength to muster his escape, he was off, and I knew he went to find his safe place.

Letting go and letting God is not as easy as it sounds. Sometimes we find ourselves treading water in pools of our own making or a pool someone else has made. Truly letting go and letting God can be possible. Through the devotions this week, I pray the Holy Spirit will guide you and help you out of your pool. I pray He will scoop you up into His net of safety. There you can breathe the fresh air of Jesus Christ. Open your heart to Him. He will *not* let you drown.

SUNDAY:

Casting all your care on Him; for he careth for you.

1 Peter 5:7 (KJV)

In this verse, we are told to *cast* (throw with force). And we are told what we are to cast. *Care.* How much? *All!* Whose? *Ours!* I thought I was to cast "the thing" on Him. But we are to cast our "care" on Him. One definition of *care* is "a troubled state of mind." Throw with force your troubled state of mind on Jesus. Do that today. Go fly fishing, and do some casting.

MONDAY:

> Again, the kingdom of heaven is like unto a net, which was cast into the sea, and gathered the good into vessels, but cast the bad away.
>
> Matthew 13:47 (KJV)

A net gave the chipmunk his life again. God's net is ready to rescue you too. Far too many times, I have felt my head jerking so as to not go under. This verse shows that you can be rescued. Think of the vastness of the sea. Then think of the net of God being "cast" into that vastness to rescue you. In the mist of the sea, you are as a speck of sand. Praise God His net is woven tight enough that you will not fall out. You don't have to struggle. All you need to do is trust in Christ. Consider writing your prayer of praise below. God loves to hear you talk to him.

TUESDAY:

> I am counted with them that go down into the pit: I am as a man that hath no strength.
>
> Psalm 88:4 (KJV)

The chipmunk tried with all of his strength to live and not drown. But what it really took was the strength of another to scoop him into the net and set him on his own feet. The same is true for you. You need only allow the Lord to scoop you up and set you on your feet. In what areas is your strength giving way? Ask God to scoop you up and give you rest.

WEDNESDAY:

> The LORD is my rock, and my fortress, and my deliverer; my God, my strength, in whom I will trust; my buckler, and the horn of my salvation, and my high tower. I will call upon the LORD, who is worthy to be praised: so shall I be saved from mine enemies."
>
> Psalm 18:1–3 (KJV)

As the chipmunk began to jerk his head, it was as if his feet just could not go anymore. We are like that when we are trying on our own. We get to a point that we cannot go on (the point where Satan wants us). Try as he might, this chipmunk's strength was failing. In Psalm 18, we are told twice that God is our strength. Refer to the last section, "saved from mine enemies." Satan would have us drown and drown in a big way, but this verse tells us that we can *call on the lord,* and be rescued. Practice calling on God today. Allow him to rescue you from your emotional, physical, and spiritual enemies.

THURSDAY:

> Bringing into captivity every thought to the obedience of Christ.
>
> 2 Corinthians 10:5 (KJV)

When you are held captive by the waters in the mist of the pool, you are unable to swim to the edge and climb out by yourself. At times, I feel I am a captive in my own world. I am being held prisoner by the indecisiveness of my heart and mind. I paddle with whatever strength I can muster. You may find the same is true for you. However, we both can bring our thoughts into captivity through His Word, and we can determine in our hearts and minds that we will obey Christ. Being imprisoned by your own mind can be a reality. Think of the ways you enslave yourself. List them and ask God to free you and refresh your soul.

FRIDAY:

So, run that ye may obtain.

2 Corinthians 9:24b (KJV)

Let us run with patience the race that is set before us,

Hebrews 12:1 (KJV)

Just as the chipmunk ran once his strength returned, you too should run that you may obtain. We must run the race that is set before us, and we each have a different race to run. The pool drained the strength from the chipmunk, but once out, he was able to continue his race. We, too, must continue our race.

SATURDAY:

> I will both lay me down in peace, and sleep: for thou, Lord, only makest me dwell in safety.
>
> Psalms 4:8 (KJV)

The chipmunk was off to safety, even though danger continued to lurk ahead. Your danger continues as well. Satan will not stop his attacks against you until your earthly life is over. You can dwell in the Lord's safety and lay down in peace and sleep. Stay in your "*safe*" place. Let go, and let *God.* Consider some dangers that could lay ahead for you. Give them over to God, and let him calm your soul.

Faith

We show faith to this world each day when we: open the closet door, flip the light switch, or turn the key in the ignition to start the car. How do you show your faith to your Father in heaven? Since faith is a noun we cannot "do" faith. We must "do" an action to show Him our faith. You showed faith, when you opened the closet door to find something there to wear, flipped the light switch trusting in the electricity, or turned the key in the ignition, faithfully believing the car would start.

SUNDAY:

> But without faith it is impossible to please Him, for he who comes to God must believe that He is, and that He is a rewarder of those who diligently seek Him.
>
> Hebrews 11:6 (NKJV)

Just how do we diligently seek Him? Here are a few ideas. We can pray or talk to Him often through out the day. We can read His words given to us divinely in the Bible. We can serve Him daily by looking for those who need Him in various ways. Bow, and ask the Lord Jesus Christ to open your eyes to an action that will show Him your faith. Be ready to act. This is one prayer He will answer quickly.

Write your request to God to make you aware of the opportunities given today which will allow you to show Him your faith.

MONDAY:

> By faith Abraham obeyed when he was called to go out to the place which he would receive as an inheritance. And he went out, not knowing where he was going.
>
> Hebrews 11:8 (NKJV)

If you don't know the story of Abraham, go to Genesis 12 and read it. It is a story you can use to get you started on this road of faith. Here was a man comfortable in his way of life. God told him, "Get out of your country." Sounds a little more than scary! But Abraham did not resist. With wife, nephew, and other family members in tow, he showed his faith and obeyed God. Ask God to show you something you can do for Him today. Then obey.

Ask Him today for forgiveness for the times He made a request of you and you did not respond. Then ask Him where He wants you to go today to do His will.

TUESDAY:

> By faith he dwelt in the land of promise as in a foreign country, dwelling in tents with Isaac and Jacob, the heirs with him of the same promise;
>
> Hebrews 11:9 (NKJV)

Sometimes our daily life puts us in a foreign land. You know the one, the place where, from the moment you awoke, nothing felt real or normal. No matter how hard you tried, you couldn't get back home, where everything is right and goes according to plan or at least to your expectations. But this day, the day you are awake in that foreign place, everything from putting butter on your toast, to answering your boss' twentieth question, has left you feeling alone. Dwell there today, but ask God to join you. The problem with a foreign land is you feel alone. God never leaves you alone. He is always there for you to call upon. The best part is: He wants you to call.

Tell God thank you for the foreign places He has provided so you might renew your faith, feel His presence, and be touched by Him.

WEDNESDAY:

> By faith Sarah herself also received strength to conceive seed, and she bore a child when she was past the age, because she judged Him faithful who had promised.
>
> Hebrews 11:11 (NKJV)

God had promised Sarah a child. Sarah bore that child because of her faith in God's promise, a child that was very important in the line of Jesus our Savior. God is no less faithful to us than He was to Sarah. He has made us countless promises in the Bible. Take hold of those promises. Judge Him to be faithful in all your needs and wants. Hold to those truths, and you will be made strong and able to receive His benefits today and tomorrow. Praise Him today for the strength He has given you, His faithfulness, and His love for you.

Write your praises today, so you can return to them another time.

THURSDAY:

> By faith the walls of Jericho fell down after they were encircled for seven days.
>
> Hebrews 11:30 (NKJV)

Jericho was a walled city in the land given to Joshua and the Israelites. The story is in Joshua starting chapter 6. Joshua had no idea how to fight these mighty men and this walled city. He and the Israelites had just barely entered the Promise Land. They were not warriors but instead wonderers. We so very often have walls that need to come down, walls that hold a myriad of mighty foes. God didn't leave Joshua to bring down the walls alone.

Read Joshua 5:13–15, and see how God sent help. He will do the same for you. Pick any wall you have. Pray and ask God to help you encircle the wall and blow your trumpet. It might take seven days, it might take longer, but God will be with you every day the wall is still up. Only by His strength can the wall come down. Only by your faith will God bring the wall down.

Write about the wall you have up and need God's help to bring down.

FRIDAY:

"By faith the harlot Rahab did not perish with those who did not believe, when she had received the spies with peace."

Hebrews 11:31 (NKJV)

When the spies came to Rahab's door, she could have turned them away. She could have told the city leaders the spies had visited her and what the spies told her. She could have done a lot of things, but what she did was "believe." She had faith God would save her and her family from the planned destruction of the city. It is by our faith we are saved through Jesus Christ, who died on the cross and rose again. If you have not accepted Him as your personal Savior, ask Him today. Ask Him to forgive your sins and become your *Adoni* (Lord and Master). He loves you and wants you to spend eternity with Him. Do not perish with others but have eternal life through Jesus Christ.

If you have never accepted Jesus as your Savior, believe Him and do it today. If you are one of Christ's followers, thank Him for the salvation He has brought you.

SATURDAY:

> Looking unto Jesus, the author and finisher of our faith, who for the joy that was set before Him endured the cross, despising the shame and has sat down at the right hand of the throne of God.
>
> Hebrews 12:2 (NKJV)

Because He loves you so much, Jesus endured the cross with joy. He is now at the right hand of God, His Father, and yours. By your faith, you will join Him in heaven. He alone authored your faith and He alone holds the finishing touches to be made to your faith. Sing His praises this day for bearing the shame of the cross and being the author and finisher of our faith.

List a few praises to Him and tell Him of your faith.

Unquenchable Love

Waterfalls are amazing to watch. Standing below it seems the water continually flows, originating from nowhere. Although I absolutely love summer, each year when the heat begins to drain my energy I yearn for a fresh waterfall. Jumping in the cool waters invigorate and energize.

I am reminded of the excitement of falling in love. The energy that flowed through my body was seemenly unquenchable. I would lay awake at night gazing at my new ring and planning my new life. There was nothing that could suppress the feeling of love in my heart.

God's love is unquenchable. When you are stressed and worried, feeling empty and even angry, the love of God will flow into your soul and invigorate your heart. Look to God this week as you refresh your spirit.

SUNDAY:

> Many waters cannot quench love, neither can the floods drown it: if a man would give all the substance of his house for love, it would utterly be condemned.
>
> Song of Solomon 8:7 (KJV)

The Song of Solomon is a wonderful book of love and everything love encompasses. I fell in love with this book while a very young preacher spoke the words with much passion. I could not help but be captivated. I realized God's love in a wonderful and exciting new way. I challenge you to take your Bible and read the entire Song of Solomon. Read it with the love and passion of God. Let His "Unquenchable Love" encompass your whole being. What ways do you see your relationship with Christ in the Song of Solomon?

MONDAY:

> Greater love hath no man than this, that a man lay down his life for his friends."
>
> John 15:13 (KJV)

John is considered a friend of God. Can you imagine what that is like? Are you a friend of God? You can be. God showed His unquenchable love by giving His Son for our sins. If you miss a friend or loved one, cuddle up to the heavenly Father. "Greater love hath no man ..." Your spirit can become dry and alone without love ... others can become dry without love also. When you cuddle up to God what friends can join you?

TUESDAY:

> Faithful are the wounds of a friend; but the kisses of an enemy are deceitful.
>
> Proverbs 27:6 (KJV)

How do you feel about friendly criticism? Do you enjoy having others tell you what they consider wrong about you, about your actions, or for that matter, anything to do with " you?" Today's verse tells a wound of a friend is *faithful.* If you are the friend to "inflict the wound," I am sure you hurt as well. Let Jesus help you. He is faithful. Pray, and ask Him. On the flip side, if you are the one that "receives the wound," call on Jesus. He will guide you through the healing process. I pray your wounds will heal to make you a stronger friend of God.

WEDNESDAY:

> But exhort one another daily, while it is called today; lest any of you be hardened through the deceitfulness of sin.
>
> Hebrews 3:13 (KJV)

I heard a message on the radio about spiritual lethargy. Let me see if I can paraphrase to you in a few sentences what the message was. There were ten virgins at the wedding feast: five prepared and five not prepared. Here is the spin that is not normally preached. If the five were so prepared, why didn't they address the fact that the other five were not? They were all part of the "wedding party." Should not they have been a help to others? Here is a point made in the sermon: When you have a really good meal and eat too much, you may desire sleep and even take a nap. Have you done this, as Christians? Are you taking a nap and forgetting that today will only be called today once. When it is over, it becomes yesterday. Unquenchable love is a love that refuses to be put out or subdued. If you are not exhorting one another, what are you doing? This verse says if you are not exhorting then we better be careful, because being hardened by deceitfulness of sin is just around the corner. While to exhort can be to lift up or spur on, it can also mean to warn or to admonish. Go out there, and exhort one another *today!*

THURSDAY:

> But whoso hath this world's good, and seeth his brother have need, and shutteth up his bowels of compassion from him, how dwelleth the love of God in him?
>
> 1 John 3:17 (KJV)

Take care to note this verse begins with "but whoso hath." You cannot give what you do not have. I know this verse says the "world's good," but think of it this way: if you have something—anything of value, including the gospel of Christ—you are to share it with others in need. How can you shut up your compassion and not give to the need of others. So many are hurting; ask for strength and compassion from Jesus. Be a witness for Him *today.*

FRIDAY:

> And to know the love of Christ, which passeth knowledge, that ye might be filled with all the fullness of God.
>
> Ephesians 3:19 (KJV)

Being filled with all the fullness of God might seem impossible on earth; nevertheless, this verse tells us that we can know the love of Christ. Knowing the love of Christ, you will be filled with His unquenchable love. Praise Him, and feel His unquenchable love deep within your soul. Know the reality of Romans 8:39: "Nor height, nor depth, nor any other creature, shall be able to separate us from the love of God, which is in Christ Jesus our Lord."

SATURDAY:

> Be ye therefore followers of God, as dear children; And walk in love, as Christ also hath loved us, and hath given himself for us an offering and a sacrifice to God for a sweet-smelling savor."
>
> Ephesians 5:1–2 (KJV)

Saturday represents the end of a workweek for most of us. Our spiritual workweek will end with our trip to heaven. At the end of my lifetime, I want to be known by God as a follower of God. Walk in God's "Unquenchable Love." As you go forward in your life, I pray you remember Song of Solomon 8:7. Is your love unquenchable? How can you stimulate your love for others?

Know

The word *know* is defined as "information firmly in the mind, firm belief in the truth of something, and to recognize differences." Throughout God's Word, we are told we can know some things. Ezekiel 37 tells of "The Valley of Dry Bones." In verse thirteen and fourteen of Ezekiel 37, the once very dry bones are told they "shall know." The heat of a long hot summer can zap your energy and leave you feeling empty and dry, wondering if any muscle for strength will ever grow back. This week, you will see a variety of verses in which you can "be firm" in your knowledge, you will see how the muscles, tendons, and skin will be refreshed and new. You *can know* God's Word.

SUNDAY:

> And I will take you to me for a people, and I will be to you a God: and ye shall know that I am the LORD your God, which bringeth you out from under the burdens of the Egyptians."
>
> Exodus 6:7 (KJV)

As you rest in Jesus today, let Him bring you out from under the burdens in your life and in your heart. You can live free and act on your freedom. Try this: replace each *you* and *ye* with your name, then replace the word "Egyptian" with each of your burdens (name them all)—God waits to bring you out of bondage. Just for reference, jot down a few of those troubles below, you will soon see them fade away.

MONDAY:

> And ye shall know the truth, and the truth shall make you free.
>
> John 8:32 (KJV)

This chapter of John began with a desire to trick. However, Jesus turned the trick into a chance to show His real purpose. The Pharisees and scribes did not want the real truth. But Jesus is the real truth. No matter what is going on in your life today, you can be sure Jesus is your truth, and He will set you free: spiritually free, emotionally free, and mentally free. Jesus is there for you. Know His truth, and be free.

TUESDAY:

> Whereas ye know not what shall be on the morrow. For what is your life? It is even a vapour, that appeareth for a little time, and then vanisheth away.
>
> James 4:14 (KJV)

May I suggest you read the entire chapter of James 4? Drawing close to God will give you the security your heart desires. Our flesh will try to use that desire for evil and enticements. God is the only one that knows our tomorrows. Pray, and leave those tomorrows in His most capable hands. Plan your future in Christ, and He will direct your path in all your tomorrows.

WEDNESDAY:

> And Joshua said, Hereby ye shall know that the living God is among you.
>
> Joshua 3:10 (KJV)

Every day, every moment, and every space, our living God is among us. How comforting to know He wants to be among you! When you are at your low, excited and happy, doing housework, yardwork, shopping, or working out at the gym—He is there. If we have accepted Christ as our Savior, then He is always among you. That is something *He* wants you to *know.* Utilitze His Word today.

THURSDAY:

Wherefore by their fruits ye shall know them.

Matthew 7:20 (KJV)

Some people just seem to constantly be judging others in how they look: what they wear, where they live, what they drive, and how they speak (just to name a few instances). Matthew, chapter seven, tells us that we do not need to be concerned with those things. If we want to know if a person is in the family of God, we are to look at their fruits. What "fruits" are you bearing today? Can others look at you and see an orchard of wonderful fruits? Or do they see barren trees? Perhaps, there is a drought going on in your life, in your orchard. Make a change today, and let others see your basket full of bountiful fruit. Let them know the new man (woman).

FRIDAY:

Then ye shall let your children know.

Joshua 4:22 (KJV)

Children are a blessing from God. Can your children look at your life and "really" know you have a relationship with Christ? Can they know you trust your future to God? This chapter tells of leaving a "reminder" for the children, so they will ask, and then they can be told how God brought the Israelites out from bondage. What reminder do your children see in you? You may not have a child but this applies to you as well. Children look at all adults. Let them *know* the Christ that lives within you.

SATURDAY:

> Ye are my witnesses, saith the LORD, and my servant whom I have chosen: that ye may know and believe me, and understand that I am he: before me there was no God formed, neither shall there be after me.
>
> Isaiah 43:10 (KJV)

In this verse, God tells us we can know and believe Him. He also says we can understand that He is God. He chose me, and He chose you. You are His witness, and it is your responsibility to be a witness for Him. When you have no strength and feel no life within, let God breathe His spirit and life into your soul. Rest in Him, and know that He is the Lord. Let the rejuvenating flow of His waterfall refresh your dry spirit.

Sleep

I am a very light sleeper, but sleep is something our bodies require. This week, let's take a look at sleep from God's Word. Join me, and let the Holy Spirit guide you.

SUNDAY:

> And the LORD caused a deep sleep to fall upon Adam, and he slept: and he took one of his ribs, and closed up the flesh instead thereof.
>
> Genesis 2:21 (KJV)

Sleeping like a baby can refer to a calm deep sleep physically. A comforting restful sleep spiritually is when you know you are where God wants you to be. The Lord caused Adam's deep sleep. When you live in a close relationship with Christ, you, too, can have "deep restful sleep." What is keeping you awake? Trust in Him each day, and you can be sure your sleep will be restful.

MONDAY:

> And when the sun was going down, a deep sleep fell upon Abram; and lo, an horror of great darkness fell upon him.
>
> Genesis 15:12 (KJV)

God had told Abram what was on the horizon. His sleep was filled with terror and his dreams were unsettled. He told Abram in his dream that his seed was going to be afflicted for 400 years. How sad to know your relatives were going to be servants/slaves for 400 years. What pain Abram must have felt. You may be sleeping, but the troubling knowledge of the future does not allow you to have 'Sunday's' sleep. You can trust God throughout your problematic times, and He will give you the sleep your body needs. Reflect how you can give your worries over to God.

TUESDAY:

> Thus I was; in the day the drought consumed me, and the frost by night, and my sleep departed from mine eyes.
>
> Genesis 31:40 (KJV)

The aggressive heat of summer's sun can use up your spiritual being. Rest does not seem to be a reality at this point. You may cry out for just a moment's calm and sleep … no sleep comes. You are consumed by your "issue." You can allow problems, concerns, or life issues to consume you, and become like a Jacob without sleep. When you turn your problems, concerns, and real life issues to Christ, you become as Adam. Your body and soul are healed through restful sleep. What things are comsuming your day and night?

WEDNESDAY:

> And I the LORD will be their God, and my servant David a prince among them; I the Lord have spoken it. And I will make with them a covenant of peace, and will cause the evil beasts to cease out of the land: and they shall dwell safely in the wilderness, and sleep in the woods. And I will make them and the places round about my hill a blessing; and I will cause the shower to come down in his season; there shall be showers of blessing.
>
> Ezekiel 34:24–26 (KJV)

I am not a camper. Sleeping in the woods is not a happy time for me. But this verse tells us having the Lord as our God; we can dwell safely in the wilderness and actually sleep in the woods. You can have this same safety and sleep in the wilderness of life's trials. The showers from the Lord's waterfall will refresh your restless spirit. Let the LORD be your God.

THURSDAY:

> How long wilt thou sleep, O sluggard? When wilt thou arise out of thy sleep?
>
> Proverbs 6:9 (KJV)

I can still hear those flip flop shoes walking down the hall in my home as a teenager. Each step caused the slipper heals to tap against the hardwood floor (Yes, Mom had heels on her slippers). She would walk down the hall and tell us it was time to arise out of sleep. There was no sleeping late on Saturday in our home. It was time to wake up. We could not be a sluggard. A sluggard is sluggish, slow, and almost lethargic. When you neglect reading your Bible and praying one day at a time, you are at risk of becoming a sluggard. Proverbs tells us it is time to wake up, and *arise out* of our sleep. Use the energy God gives you, and press forward with His strength. In what areas are you attempting to sleep late?

FRIDAY:

> When thou liest down, thou shalt not be afraid: yea, thou shalt lie down, and thy sleep shall be sweet.
>
> Proverbs 3:24 (KJV)

Being alone on a dark and dreary night with only the quiet of nature can be scary to some. There are people who might consider courage to mean you are never afraid. You can have the courage of Christ. When you have His bravery, you will not be afraid. You can lie down and have a wonderful, sweet sleep. Sleep can resemble your favorite "sweet treat." Accept the courage of Christ. Lie down, and wake up with a sweet smile on your face. Muse on the refreshing times God has allowed you to be gallant.

SATURDAY:

> And Jacob awaked out of his sleep, and he said, "Surely the LORD is in this place; and I knew it not.'"
>
> Genesis 28:16 (KJV)

Jacob had been sent out by his father to find a bride. It was a long journey, and Jacob stoped to find a place to lay his head. He struggled all night long and woke to realize in the midst of his battle the LORD was with him. You go through your days and nights with trials, tribulations, questions, and concerns. You can struggle and fight, but toiling and warring will be to no avail. Lay your needs and desires in the almighty hand of God. Awaken out of your sleep, and trust in Him today. *He will* perform that which He desires in you.

Ultimate Sacrifice

We have several federal holidays to remember our military. Men and women have given their lives for the freedom of the United States of America, as well as protecting around the globe. They are literally offering to lay down their lives. Jesus tells us there is no greater love (John 15:13). Christ made the ultimate sacrifice for all. His life was given to pay the sin debt for all. Sacrifice is to give up something of value. You go through many activities each day interacting with others. Within those interactions someone is forgoing their personal "self." In everyday life we make choices. Do you give of yourself or require the other person to give in? Let's consider our sacrifice this week.

SUNDAY:

> We will go three days' journey into the wilderness, and sacrifice to the LORD our God, as he shall command us.
>
> Exodus 8:27 (KJV)

Sacrifice as a noun means "an act of offering to a deity." Sacrifice as a verb means "to make or perform." Moses pled with Pharaoh to sacrifice to the LORD. He would not give in to Pharaoh and sacrifice within the Egyptian's homeland. Moses would not compromise the instruction the Lord had given him. Do you compromise the instruction God gives you? Leave the bondage of your Egypt. Resist the desire to concede. Take time today, and ask God to help you stand strong and the instructions He gives to you. Can you sacrifice and dispel negotiations tempting your heart?

MONDAY:

> This is my commandment, that ye love one another, as I have loved you.
>
> John 15:12 (KJV)

Having a friend is very special. When you are a friend, you are charged with a very serious responsibility. What are your motives as a friend? Do you have time for your friends? Do you sacrifice your personal desires for the needs of your friends? Through the strength and guidance of the Holy Spirit, you can be a true friend and love as He loves you. Is your personal desire for you or your friends?

TUESDAY:

> I exhort therefore, that, first of all, supplications, prayers, intercessions, and giving of thanks, be made for all men.
>
> 1 Timothy 2:1 (KJV)

Jesus called us "friend" throughout the New Testament. We have the privilege of "prayer and supplication." Jesus spent many hours in prayer. Take time today to follow His example and sacrifice some of your time in prayer for your friends and family. Making a list is a good way to stay on focus during your prayer time.

WEDNESDAY:

> Seek the LORD and his strength, seek his face continually. Remember his marvelous works that he hath done, his wonders, and the judgments of his mouth."
>
> 1 Chronicles 16:11–12 (KJV)

Here we are at midweek, and for many, this is considered "hump day" (the day we have reached the top of the hill). Are you on the tip of the hump and ready for a downhill slide? This can signify a time of ease. During your "time of ease," remember His marvelous works, His wonders, and the wonderful judgments of His mouth! Let Him love you to a pleasant calm of heart.

THURSDAY:

> Wherefore seeing we also are compassed about with so great a cloud of witnesses, let us lay aside every weight, and the sin which doth so easily best us, and let us run with patience the race that is set before us."
>
> Hebrews 12:1 (KJV)

Men and women of the military are quick to learn they must follow orders. They must also lay aside every weight that may cause them or their squad harm. Their focus must be on the situation at hand. As Christians, we, too, must learn to lay aside those weights and even the sin that plagues our very soul. God has a plan for your life. Run your race with patience. What is weighing you down? Draw on God's Word to relax and calm your spirit.

FRIDAY:

> Looking unto Jesus the author and finisher of our faith; who for the joy that was set before him endured the cross, despising the shame, and is set down at the right hand of the throne of God.
>
> Hebrews 12:2 (KJV)

Sometimes, we feel as if we cannot endure our situation. This verse shows that the ultimate endurance was made by the author and finisher of our faith: Jesus Christ. Once the ultimate sacrifice was made, Jesus set down at the right hand of the throne of God. Nearing the last day of the week, our stamina wains and we wonder, can we go on? Ask God to help you stay the course and be presistant in your walk with Him.

SATURDAY:

> For God so loved the world that he gave his only begotten son, that whosoever believeth in him should not perish, but have everlasting life.
>
> John 3:16 (KJV)

Giving of yourself, personally can sometimes be a hard task. What would it be like to "give" your child the charge of carring the sin of the world and then having to turn your back on that "only" child? God made an ultimate sacrifice in giving his only son. He made that sacrifice for you. Join me in pledging today to follow God and strive to show others they too can have everlasting life with Him. Are you giving?

PART III

autumn

Life's changing colors are revealed using God's Plan.

AUTUMN

A coolness in the breeze
Tells of changes in the air.
Just what trials may abound,
And do I care?

Colors surround me as do needs.
All becomes shades of grey
And my depression it feeds.

He holds my tether full of hope.
By His Word, I find my rope.
His grasp on me is ever tight.
He received all of me
When He fought that fight.

As years have passed, I love Him more,
Thinking often of the cross He bore.
From dusk till dawn, I will sing His praise,
Because it was for me, from death He raised.

—Kathleen J. Jones—

Just as the leaves change from the healthy green cool colors to deep red, orange, and golden yellow warm colors, a variety of trials span throughout the lives of the young teen to the busy coed, from the unwed parent to the career traveler, and from the newlywed through to the great-grandparent. Those cool colors relax and calm while the warm shades tend to give a feeling of closing in and being confined. Trials can cause us to dwell on the negatives of life. And yet the warm hues can give us the cozy and cuddling security of a deep love that will come to life as we rely on God's Word. Relax and enjoy each new day, as autumn's devotions bring you to a closer relationship with Christ.

Adoration of Our Holy Father

Adoration can mean affection, love, passion, worship, devotion, or idolatry. When the negatives of life, those times when things are gray instead of filled with color, seem to engulf your very soul, let these devotions bring the "Adoration of Your Holy Father" to fruition and reproduce the colors of red and gold and orange back into your days. Lift your voice and hands in praise.

SUNDAY:

> Delight yourself also in the Lord, and He shall give you the desires of your heart.
>
> Psalm 37:4 (NKJV)

Has God told us He will give us anything we want in today's scripture? Yes and No! Yes, if we delight ourselves in the Lord our desires then change and if our focus is on God we become more in tune to His desires for us. The more often you seek him by prayer and reading His word, the more closely you will listen for what is right and what fits into His plan. Show Him your true affection today by asking for the desires of His heart to become your desires. Listen for His response, and then go forward.

Journal not only your praises to Him but what you believe His response is.

MONDAY:

> Therefore take careful heed to yourselves that you love the Lord your God.
>
> Joshua 23:11 (NKJV)

When we truly love someone, our actions show it. We try to make life easier for them in every way. We listen to their advice. We accept their knowledge of a particular experience. We more readily accept their help in certain areas of life. The same is true with your love for your Holy Father. The more you love Him, the more closely you will listen to His advice and accept His way of doing things. He has made a plan for you. Ask him to show you His plan and then respond to it.

Journal what you believe His plan for you is today.

TUESDAY:

> And being found in appearance as a man, He humbled Himself and became obedient to the point of death, even the death of the cross.
>
> Philippians 2:8 (NKJV)

What are you passionate about? Does chocolate, coffee, children, spouse, or shopping come to mind? Would you die for your passion? Jesus did. He had only one passion. That passion was leaving heaven, becoming a man, and following the will of His Father to die on the cross. Because Jesus followed His passion, He now sits at the right hand of God. Make your passion the Holy Father and His will for you. Your rewards will be incomprehensible.

Journal your passion and just how that fits into God's plan. Will following your passion bring the bright colors back into your life?

WEDNESDAY:

> So Moses made haste and bowed his head toward the earth and worshiped.
>
> Exodus 34:8 (NKJV)

Bowing our head is a good place to begin when worshiping the Lord. To carry the journey forward, we must set our hearts toward our destinations. Having a right heart will change your attitude. Turning your attitudes, we will replace old actions with new ones. Actions show our true worship of the Father. Bow your head today, move your heart, navigate your attitude, and act upon your Lord's wishes.

What attitudes have been changed today by bowing your head?

THURSDAY:

> Peter answered and said to Him, "Even if all are made to stumble because of You, I will never be made to stumble.'"
>
> Matthew 26:33 (NKJV)

And yet, we know Peter did stumble. But his devotion to Christ was always deep within. Jesus knew what was about to happen and cautioned Peter about the events. When the Roman guards came for Jesus, Peter panicked and went the way of everyone else. After Jesus rose again, He went personally to Peter and forgave him. We, like Peter, sometimes let our "happenings" get in front of our devotion to Christ. This is what can cause the grays to appear in our lives. Ask His forgiveness for any time you may have failed to let your devotion to Him control all your "happenings" rather than He being in control.

FRIDAY:

You shall have no other gods before me.

Exodus 20:3 (NKJV)

This is the first commandment given to Moses. It is our first commandment today. But some of the "gods" we bow to today are: television, jobs, comforts we enjoy, children, or husbands. Though we owe Him everything from life itself to the everlasting life with Him, we still put other things before Him. Spend time today putting aside all those "gods," and put Him first in all you do or say. Jesus is all the colors of our lives no matter how many things may get in the way.

Confess to Him some of the other gods you have allowed to control you life.

SATURDAY:

> You shall love the Lord your God with all your heart, with all your soul, and with all your strength.
>
> Deuteronomy 6:5 (NKJV)

Loving the Lord your God with heart, soul, and strength is to put Him first in every thought and deed. To do this, you must first offer Him your independence. Giving Him your independence does not mean you will be waiting on the sidelines with nothing to do. On the contrary, it means He can put you to work right away because He knows where you are to go and how you are to get there. Ask Him to direct all your paths, speech, and thoughts. Give Him your adoration with your deeds and your words.

Put the color back into your adoration by telling Him how your deeds and thoughts will change with Him in mind at all times.

Prosperity

When you hear the words *prosperity* or *prosperous,* does your mind automatically think *money?* We can be prosperous in many ways, only one of which includes our money. In reading God's Word, we will find ways He is the God of prosperity. And that same prosperity is inclusive with His provisions. We will also find what He expects us to do with the prosperity of the provisions He brings to us.

SUNDAY:

> "Please take my blessing that is brought to you, because God has dealt graciously with me, and because I have enough." So he urged him and he took it."
>
> Genesis 33:11 (NKJV)

These are words spoken by Jacob to Esau upon Jacob's return to his homeland. Remember, Jacob had fled after having taken Esau's blessing deceitfully. While away, Jacob had become very rich. He was rich in money, wives, flocks, and his relationship with God. God had blessed him substantially. When Jacob returned, he gave Esau a sizable portion of his money, flocks, and household goods. Take stock of all you have this week. Is there a portion you might share?

List some of the prosperity God has afforded you.

MONDAY:

> Unless the Lord builds the house, they labor in vein who build it, unless the Lord guards the city, the watchman stays awake in vain.
>
> Psalm 127:1 (NKJV)

Are you trying to build your prosperity without God? His words cannot be any plainer. If you are trying to do anything without His blessings, it just won't work out the way it should. I agree, there are those very prosperous that have nothing to do with God, but if we were allowed a close look into their daily lives, we might not find things so "happily ever after." Include the Father in your plans for prosperity, whether those plans be building a house or guarding all you currently have.

What provisions has God made for you today?

TUESDAY:

> In the day of prosperity be joyful, but in the day of adversity consider: Surely God has appointed the one as well as the other, so that man can find out nothing that will come after him.
>
> Ecclesiastes 7:14 (NKJV)

By God's design, we have prosperity and adversity. Which ever you are in the midst of at this time, know the other will occur. God set it up that way. There have been times I have been in the midst of both at the same time. Maybe my money was doing great, but my family or friendship life was so out of whack I wondered, if I would make it through. We have so many facets to our lives; it is imperative we consider each facet before deciding if He has placed us in a waste and or if He has set us on the mountaintop.

List the different facets of your life then count them on the mountaintop or in the valley.

WEDNESDAY:

> The more they increased, the more they sinned against Me;
> I will change their glory into shame."
>
> Hosea 4:7 (NKJV)

One reason God may not have increased your prosperity to its full potential is the verse above. The more God gave the Israelites, the more they sinned against His will. Check yourself on just how you are responding to the prosperity God has brought you. If you are sure there is *no* prosperity in your life, ask yourself, "How have I responded to God in the past?"

Remind yourself if there are provisions God has made for you that you might not have used to His glory.

THURSDAY:

> When they had pasture they were filled; they were filled and their heart was exalted; therefore they forgot Me."
>
> Hosea 13:6 (NKJV)

A very real danger in prosperity is that it can lead to abandoning our relationship with Christ. We get so busy in the "more and more" business, we do not take the time to build the prosperity in our relationship with God. Our time becomes filled more and more with work, family, friends, and whatever we can find to take time away from the one who really loves us. Set aside time today, and every day, to make your relationship with the Father and Son prosperous.

Tell yourself where you will find some much needed time each day to make your relationship with God more prosperous. Remember, He makes the provision for even this.

FRIDAY:

> Now it came to pass, when Rehoboam had established the kingdom and had strengthened himself, that he forsook the law of the Lord, and all Israel along with him.
>
> 2 Chronicles 12:1 (NKJV)

When we get so sure of where we are and how we are doing, it isn't just ourselves that can be pulled away from God and what He has for us. We all hold some kind of leadership responsibility, maybe it is as a parent or worker or spouse. Others are watching what and how you do what you do. Don't become a Rehoboam, and take the entire country down with you! Lift your attitude toward your prosperity to Christ today—let Him help you.

SATURDAY:

> But when he was strong his heart was lifted up, to his destruction, for he transgressed against the Lord his God by entering the temple of the Lord to burn incense on the altar of incense.
>
> 2 Chronicles 26:16 (NKJV)

Uzziah became king at the age of sixteen. He did many great things for more than just Israel. He was so well known, kings from other lands brought him gifts. Remember the scripture "pride goeth before the fall?" Uzziah became so prosperous in all areas of his life, but one, his relationship with God. He felt equal to perform what God had commanded only the high priest could do. Be careful with your pride. Always remember where all prosperity and provisions comes from! Go with God and His Son Jesus Christ this week, and fill your bowls full of prosperity, but remember where it came from.

Write your thanks to God for the provisions He has set aside for you this week.

Directions

There are times we want to know exactly how to get from A to Z. We are now in the technology age where we can pull up maps on the Internet or possibly we have a GPS in our cars. For those of us that do not know what a GPS is: Basically, it is a small computer showing the best way to get from A to Z. However, we have always had our *GPS, "God Paved Streets."* When lifes trials close in and we need some help finding our way, we can use our heavenly GPS. Spend this week looking at the directions God has given you to travel "His" paved streets.

SUNDAY:

For I know the plans I have for you declares the Lord.

Jeremiah 29:11 (NIV)

God has already set your directions in place. His word tells you, He knows His plans for you. They are not the same plans for all. We each have our own streets we are to take. Avenues paved by God. Today, pray for Him to show you the direction He wants you to go.

MONDAY:

> The Lord had said to Abram "Leave your country, your people and your father's household and go to the land I will show you."
>
> Genesis 11:27 (NIV)

Sometimes your directions are not complete. You must take each step one at a time. God did not give Abram the complete path he was to take all at one time. He said, "Go where I show you." You can use your faith to follow the paved street, because you know who paved the street. Do you have paths that need rerouted?

TUESDAY:

> The word of the Lord came to Jonah son of Amittal; "Go to the great city of Nineveh and preach against it, because its wickedness has come up before me." But Jonah ran away from the Lord and headed for Tarshish
>
> Jonah 1:1–3a (NIV)

Sometimes you know exactly where you are to go. God has given you the complete direction, each and every street, every turn, and even what you are to do once you get there. But you disobey and run from Him. Could it be you are afraid of what you must do, or like Jonah, you disagree with why or what He has planned for you. Do not be afraid to follow His street. Have faith in God. He knows much more about your capabilities.

WEDNESDAY:

> Moses my servant is dead. Now then, you and all these people get ready to cross the Jordan River into the land I am about to give to them --to the Israelites.
>
> Joshua 1:2 (NIV)

Be clear in the direction God is sending you. Get ready to go, and do what He is telling you to do. Make certain you understand where, when, and how you are to take your step. Ask Him for the plan. He may only give you the first part, but that is the beginning, and that may be all you need for that moment. Just as the color of the leaves change in autumn, our direction can change from calm and healthy to chaos and stress. Practice following God one step at a time.

THURSDAY:

> Have I not commanded you? Be strong and courageous. Do not be terrified; do not be discouraged for the Lord your God will be with you wherever you go.
>
> Joshua 1:9 (NIV)

Be confident that wherever God is sending you, you will be able to fulfill His plan. He has created you with abilities you need, and He will be with you. He has not given you these abilities to waste. Use them for His glory. You will be glad you did. Your relationship with God will deepen and the love you have for him will become stronger. Cuddle up and trust His plan.

FRIDAY:

> Do not let this book of the law depart from your mouth; meditate on it day and night, so that you may be careful to do everything written in it. Then you will be prosperous and successful.
>
> Joshua 1:8 (NIV)

There are times you might want to take a turn away from God's path. Be aware of the stop signs and turns calling out to you. Avoid them by knowing and being in His Word daily. He will help you avoid the pit falls. Following God's path brings prosperity and success. Do you see any signs that call out to you? Are they taking you away from God's path? List them below and pray for strength to avoid wrong turns.

SATURDAY:

> Get your supplies ready. Three days from now you will cross the Jordan here to go in and take possession of the land the Lord your God is giving you for your own.
>
> Joshua 1:11b (NIV)

Get ready and go. Pick up what you need to take, and commit yourself to the work God has for you. He is waiting for you to accept His plan for your life. Begin traveling on "God-Paved Streets." God's provision is always sure and safe. Follow his GPS and live a life full of hope and love.

Words

Day Light Savings brings changes to our outside world. Could this be a time we should be looking toward making changes to our inside world. The changes in the outside world are temperature and colors from greens to several shades of red. Inside we may have trials asking us to change how we look at life. What about the words we use? Do we use words that build us up or words that bring us further into the trials of life? This week we will look at words that can bring us back to the hope God provides for us.

SUNDAY:

> Don't you know that when you offer yourselves to someone to obey him as slaves, you are slaves to the one whom you obey-whether you are slaves to sin which leads to death, or to obedience which leads to righteousness?
>
> Romans 6:16 (NIV)

Obedience is defined as the "act or practice of following instructions, complying with rules or regulations, or submitting to someone's authority." Referring to the scripture above, to whose authority are you submitting yourself? Are you submitting yourself to the regulations or rules of the world outside, or are you allowing the Holy Spirit to give you instructions? Do you take the instructions and comply, or do you take the easy way and go with the world? Today, before you make a decision small or large, ask the Holy Spirit to guide you. Allow Him to give you instruction and comply with His authority. He knows where the decision will lead.

List some of the decisions He has helped you make. Praise Him for those paths He has put you on.

MONDAY:

> Commit your way to the Lord; trust in Him and He will do this; He will make your righteousness shine like the dawn, the justice of your cause like the noonday sun.
>
> Psalm 37:5–6 (NIV)

Commitment is loyalty, devotion, or dedication. Commitment to the Lord has its rewards, as does a commitment to the outside world. Committing your way to the Father will allow the righteousness within you to shine like the morning dawn. This is a brightness that allows a new beginning each day, no matter what the day before may have hidden. His justice shines like the noonday sun. He went to the cross for you, so you would not live in darkness. Today, commit all of yourself to the Lord, not just your heart, but all of your ways—your complete life. He will shine through you today no matter what darkness lurks around you.

What are those hidden trials? Write them below so God's righteousness will be revealed and His light will shine.

TUESDAY:

> The day is Yours, and Yours also the night; You established the sun and moon. It was You who set all the boundaries of the earth; You made both summer and winter."
>
> Psalm 74:16–17 (NIV)

Boundaries are limits, the point at which something ends. Have you set your own limits, or do you allow God to set them for you? Are you living in your own comfortable land, or are you stepping out in faith? He set the boundaries of this world. Our scripture tells you He established the sun and the moon. He knows whether you can survive the cold winter or the heat of the summer. Allow Him to set your limits. Step out in faith today, and cross over the boundaries you have drawn. He will keep you in the warmth of His winter and the cool of His summer.

What boundary have you set for yourself that God is asking you to step beyond? Write it below, and show God your faith in Him.

WEDNESDAY:

> O Lord, God of our fathers Abraham, Isaac and Israel, keep this desire in the hearts of your people forever, and keep their hearts loyal to you.
>
> 1 Chronicles 29:18 (NIV)

Loyalty is a feeling of devotion. As you read the words "a feeling of devotion," do they create a desire in your heart to jump up and praise the Lord? The writer is appealing to the Lord to keep the yearning for Him in the hearts of his people forever. The appeal includes to be ever devoted and to serve Him forever. Do you yearn for this desire? Take time, and ask Your Father to put this desire in your heart. Be steadfast, dedicated, and faithful to Him who is always faithful to you.

Today use the area below to show your desire to be steadfast, dedicated, and faithful to your Father.

THURSDAY:

If it is leadership let him govern diligently.

Romans 12:8 (NIV)

Leadership is the ability to guide, direct, or influence people. To be diligent is to show persistent and hard-working effort in doing something. You may not think of yourself as a leader, but God knows when He wants you to lead. This scripture speaks of the gift of leadership. There are times when God gives you the leadership ability to show others His ways and direct them to Him. Just as we spoke of boundaries earlier, the time may be right for you to direct the path of a loved one to Him. Ask Him today to show you if this is that moment in time. If now is the time, He will give you this ability. Then go for it with diligence for The Lord.

Write the names of loved ones you would like to lead to Christ. Pray over those names, and ask God to show you when He would have you speak to them.

FRIDAY:

Be prepared in season and out of season.

2 Timothy 4:2 (NIV)

Being prepared is to be ready beforehand or to put together in advance. Yesterday, we spoke of leadership; today know He has prepared this day for you. He knows where this day will lead. Allow Him to prepare you for each event that will take place today. You will be allowed to experience a day of learning and growing as you have never before. Remember, He set the day beforehand. He made it ready for you. Now allow Him to ready you.

Thank Him for preparing you for this day, use the lines below.

SATURDAY:

> Let the beloved of the LORD rest secure in him, for he shields him all day long, and the one the LORD loves rests between his shoulders.
>
> Deuteronomy 33:12 (NIV)

Security is the state or feeling of being safe and protected, freedom from worries. Do you rest in the security of the Lord? Do you feel safe and protected or free from the worries of each day? Today, give those worries to Him; allow Him to shield you all day long. Relax, know you are the beloved of the Father, and rest between *his* shoulders.

Use the area below to write out those worries and then give them over to God.

A Week of Thanksgiving

There are times in our lives when the only thing to do is lift praise and thanksgiving to our Lord Jesus Christ. Often, we feel inept at just what to say to get our feelings across, especially when we are in a time of trial and frustration. I have found the best way to say what I want to say is to turn to the Scriptures, and pray them to God. For this week, take each scripture, write it on a card or a piece of paper, and carry it with you. During any lull in your day, pull out the scripture, and say it allowed in an attitude of prayer.

Remember to write your first thoughts of the scripture in the reflection section of each day. Praise Him often and honestly.

SUNDAY:

I will praise You, O Lord, with my whole heart; I will tell of all Your marvelous works. I will be glad and rejoice in You; I will sing praise to Your name, O Most High.

Psalm 9:1–2 (NKJV)

MONDAY:

I will sing to the Lord, because He has dealt bountifully with me.

Psalm 13:6 (NKJV)

TUESDAY:

That I may proclaim with the voice of thanksgiving, and tell of all Your wondrous works, Lord. I have loved the habitation of Your house, and the place where Your glory dwells.

Psalm 26:7–8 (NKJV)

WEDNESDAY:

Many, O Lord my God, are Your wonderful works which You have done; and Your thoughts toward us cannot be recounted to You in order; if I would declare and speak of them, they are more than can be numbered.

Psalm 40:5 (NKJV)

THURSDAY:

It is good to give thanks to the Lord, and to sing praises to Your name, O Most High; to declare Your loving-kindness in the morning, and Your faithfulness every night … For You, Lord, have made me glad through Your work; I will triumph in the works of Your hands.

Psalm 92:1, 2, 4 (NKJV)

FRIDAY:

Oh, sing to the Lord a new song! For He has done marvelous things; His right hand and His holy arm have gained Him the victory.

Psalm 98:1 (NKJV)

SATURDAY:

Oh, give thanks to the Lord, for He is good! For His mercy endures forever. Oh, give thanks to the God of gods! For His mercy endures forever. Oh, give thanks to the Lord of lords! For His mercy endures forever.

Psalm 136: 1–3 (NKJV)

Hezekiah—Added Days

Autumn is the time of year in which various trees and plants loose their foliage. The veins carrying the nutrients close, and do not allow water and sap to flow through to the folige. They do not get to wait one more month or one more year. Although this process happens again, the leaves that do drop off are gone, never to grow back.

As I watched the leaves fall to the ground in my own yard, I thanked God that he gave me added days. The stresses of life may tend to get you down. Your spiritual veins may close and nutrients are no longer providing the energy you need. The why of your autumn is not what is important. Realize that winter is coming. Autumn is a required season for prepration for the colder days ahead. Hezekiah served the Lord and asked for "added days." Muse on each days verse, and cuddle up to God, knowing that He will comfort you and prepare you for the cold winter ahead.

SUNDAY:

> In those days was Hezekiah sick unto death. And the prophet Isaiah the son of Amoz came to him, and said unto him, "Thus saith the LORD, Set thine house in order; for thou shalt die, and not live."
>
> 2 Kings 20:1 (KJV)

There comes a time when order is necessary. As a compulsive list maker, order is part of my everyday life. But I have friends, who never have order show up at their doorsteps. The order in this scripture was directed by God to Hezekiah. He was sick unto death, as the word comes from Isaiah, and Hezekiah knew this was serious. We can live every day with our house in order. Talk to God about your house (physical and emotional as well as your "household.") He will help you, and direct you to set your house in order today.

MONDAY:

> Then he turned his face to the wall, and prayed unto the Lord, saying, "I beseech thee, O Lord, remember now how I have walked before thee in truth and with a perfect heart, and have done that which is good in thy sight." And Hezekiah wept sore.
>
> 2 Kings 20:2–3 (KJV)

Nights and days pass; weeping seems as if it will never subside. Then one day, you feel the presence of God, and you are able to dry some of those tears and freshen up. Hezekiah knew the right person to pray to. Verse three says it all: "I beseech thee, O Lord." It is important that we know whom to beseech. Loved ones can be a great help, because they are there in the flesh, but when we are deep in pain, we need the supernatural help that only God can give. Call on Him today for yourself or a loved one. Be warm and secure in His arms.

TUESDAY:

> Remember now how I have walked before thee in truth and with a perfect heart, and have done that which is good in thy sight.
>
> 2 Kings 20:3 (KJV)

When Hezekiah prayed to God, he reminded God of what he "had" done and how he "had" acted. I cannot help but wonder how God really felt about the "have" done. God has such a wonderful love for us that I am sure He smiled and remembered the joy He felt while Hezekiah walked in the truth, had a perfect heart, and even did well in the sight of God. That pleasantry must have caused God to smile, and thus, He "added the days." You too, can make God smile. Even though lifes changing situtations can cause you to stumble and maybe even turn cold, you can be an everyday part of God's smile.

WEDNESDAY:

> And it came to pass, afore Isaiah was gone out into the middle court, that the word of the LORD came to him, saying, Turn again, and tell Hezekiah the captain of my people, Thus saith the LORD, the God of David thy father, "I have heard thy prayer."
>
> 2 Kings 20:4–5a (KJV)

Here is one example of proof that God will hear your prayers. Hezekiah prayed unto the Lord, and Isaiah did not even have time to leave the courtyard before God told him to turn around, and go back to tell Hezekiah the Lord heard him. Amazing! Maybe your prayers don't always get answered that fast, but they can be. Rest in the knowledge that God wants to hear our prayers. Go to him today. Let Him say to you, "I have heard thy prayer." Write a prayer thanking God for answered prayer.

THURSDAY:

I have seen thy tears.

2 Kings 20:5 (KJV)

I have had my fair share of tear-filled nights that NO one saw or knew. How did I get through? Because I knew God saw my tears. I knew God cared about every tear that seeped from my eyes. When I had cried so much that tears refused to come, God still saw my tears. He will see your tears too. The pain in your soul can only be healed by our wonderful God. Don't be afraid to let *him* see. He already knows and wants to comfort you.

FRIDAY:

Behold, I will heal thee.

2 Kings 20:5 (KJV)

Let an all knowing, all-powerful God heal you. Times can seem so very hard. You may need emotional healing, physical healing, and spiritual healing. No one can heal like your Savior. Hezekiah was sick unto *death.* In whatever way you relate to Hezekiah's situation, *allow God to heal you.*

SATURDAY:

> On the third day thou shalt go up unto the house of the Lord. And I will add unto thy days fifteen years; and I will deliver thee and this city out of the hand of the king of Assyria; and I will defend this city for mine own sake, and for my servant David's sake. And Isaiah said, "Take a lump of figs. And they took and laid it on the boil, and he recovered."
>
> 2 Kings 20:6–7 (KJV)

Do you ask the question: "Why did God heal Hezekiah?" Besides the fact that he heard his prayer and saw his tears, why did God heal Hezekiah, as well as deliver him? Check out verse six, God wants you to see and know *His majesty!* He says, "for mine own sake, and for my servant David's sake." God made a promise, and *He* keeps *His* promises. If you read the rest of this story, you will see that Hezekiah became very selfish in his thinking, and God knew that was on the horizon; yet He still healed him. This gives me the thought that it really wasn't for Hezekiah's sake that God healed him. It was to show God's own Majesty. We are not here for "us." Although we are God's children, and He loves us, this whole earthly experience is about God and God showing *His majesty.* Be a part of that showing, and tell others about *Him.* Let others see God in your *everyday* life, and every "added day" you have, live for Christ.

A Way of Life

For this week, we are going to Matthew chapter five, and dig deep about what Jesus had to say about our every day life. He talked to the people about the provisions God had made for their lives and how to rely on God in every situation. Of course, Jesus was talking in ancient times, but all He ever said is relevant today. His truths were relevant then, they are relevant today, and they will be relevant as long as He allows us to have tomorrows.

SUNDAY:

> For assuredly, I say to you, till heaven and earth pass away, one jot or one tittle will by no means pass from the law till all is fulfilled.
>
> Matthew 5:18 (NKJV)

Thousands of people protest living under the law. There are laws of nature, laws of man, and laws of God. Think for a moment what life would be like if we had no laws.

Did your mind refuse to go any further when you got to the first mass chaos? Mine did. Jesus is telling us we can change anything anytime, but all God has previously said will come true. Praise God today for His laws and all His promises of fulfillment.

If we were to follow God's law of love, how would our lives change?

MONDAY:

> But I say to you that whoever is angry with his brother without a cause shall be in danger of the judgment.
>
> Matthew 5:22a (NKJV)

Know someone with a habit that just pricks at you every time you are around them? Maybe it is an action, or maybe a sound they make, or maybe something they say. It could be something you believe they should change in their life, but instead they just keep complaining about it. But it doesn't matter what the prick to you is. Jesus says if we are angry with our brother (or sister) for just being who they are, it is to our detriment. Bow today, and ask the Father to forgive you. Then go, and ask your brother or sister for their forgiveness. Chances are they didn't even realize they were bothering you. This may seem like a small challenge instead of a tough trial. But it is often the small things in life that cause us to sin against one another.

Write some of things you believe to be small challenges but still cause tough trials.

TUESDAY:

> But I say to you that whoever looks at a woman to lust for her has already committed adultery with her in his heart.
>
> Matthew 5:28 (NKJV)

Jesus addressed how men were looking at women, but this door swings both ways. If a female has seen some hunk and wondered what he would be like in the sack, then you are as guilty as the men of which Jesus spoke. There are other lusts we must control too. Sometimes, we lust for jewelry, a large home, a new vehicle, lots of money, or closets full of clothes. All these lusts can bring destruction. They may cause us to lie and cheat in ways we would never have considered before. Watch where and on what you set your mind to thinking. Kneel, and ask Jesus for forgiveness. Then ask Him to put your thoughts on Him.

List something you have been lusting over, but now see it caused its own trial.

WEDNESDAY:

> But I say to you that whoever divorces his wife for any reason except sexual immorality causes her to commit adultery; and whoever marries a woman who is divorced commits adultery.
>
> Matthew 5:32 (NKJV)

Divorce is thought to be a way of life in today's society. But that is not how God planned it. If this is something that has happened to you, I am truly sorry. There never has been a "good" divorce. It hurts to the deepest core. And it hurts our Father in heaven even more deeply. But our heavenly Father can heal you and make you well. He can and will choose your next partner. Give yourself time to heal and time for Him to point you in the right direction. Spend your waiting time in His word with His people. Thank Him today for bringing you through.

Write to your Father some of the trials He brought you through, or if not you, someone you know who had been through divorce.

THURSDAY:

> But let your "Yes" be "Yes" and your "No" be "No." For whatever is more than these is from the evil one.
>
> Matthew 5:37 (NKJV)

Wouldn't it be wonderful in this life if we could trust one another so much we could do away with contracts and courts? But of course, we cannot. There are those in this world who will cheat just because they can. But you don't have to be one of them. If you say you will do something, do it. Take the responsibility of keeping your word. Both yes and no-hold responsibility. You just have to figure out which one is the right one for the moment. Ask your Father before you answer with yes or no. He will give you the correct reply for every situation. He knows your tomorrows, and only He knows which things you can and cannot do.

Commit below to God to make your yes be yes and your no be no. By His provision you will lessen the trial of a wavering answer.

FRIDAY:

> Give to him who asks you, and from him who wants to borrow from you do not turn away.
>
> Matthew 5:42 (NKJV)

There are those of us who are especially good at giving. Then, there are those of us who always think twice before we let go. Jesus says give to those who ask, and do not turn away those who want to borrow. The truth is we cannot out give Jesus. If we will just let go and give what others might need, He will provide more than we need. He will fill our cup to overflowing. It is one of His many promises to us. So let go today, give to someone who asks, and do not turn away. Thank Jesus for the opportunity to show His love to someone else. Even in times of financial need, God will provide what you are asked to give.

List what He may be asking you to give even though you might be in a financial bind at the moment.

SATURDAY:

> But I say to you, love your enemies, bless those who curse you, do good to those who hate you, and pray for those who spitefully use you and persecute you.
>
> Matthew 5:44 (NKJV)

This may be the hardest of Jesus' teachings to perform on a day-by-day basis. When we have been hurt, either physically or emotionally, it is difficult to lift the person who hurt us to the Lord. But that is exactly what Jesus tells us to do. If you can learn to do this, there is a two-fold blessing for you. First, lifting that person up just may be the thing that brings him or her to the saving power of Jesus Christ. That person will not understand your reaction to the pain caused and could very well ask you why you reacted the way you did. If so, you have the perfect opportunity to speak of your Savior. Second, by lifting that person up to God and forgiving the injustice done to you, God provides a salve to you. He is your balm. He will heal the hurt and draw you closer to Him.

Ask Him today to help you pray for someone who has hurt you in the past.

From the Cross

From the beginning, Jesus' total concern has been for you and me. The cross was His darkest hour, and His most glorious hour (until His second coming). Even though He knew how His thirty-three years on earth would end, the last twenty-four hours of His life left Him saddened and wanting. But He also knew to call on His Father in times of need. This week, we will spend our time learning from Him how to spend our most "wanting" moments.

SUNDAY:

> Father, forgive them for they do not know what they do. And they divided His garments and cast lots.
>
> Luke 23:34 (NKJV)

His time on the cross was spent not about Himself but about forgiveness. Jesus was not just physically in pain on the cross, but from His words, we can believe His heart was breaking over what He knew was coming for this human race. Jesus saw the deepest hurts people would cause and where those hurts would lead. In dividing His garments, the soldiers removed every symbol of His life as a man. But amidst their evil deeds, Jesus opened the door to their salvation. Should there be people you know who are doing their best to bring their lives to ruin, pray God will forgive them for what they do not know they do.

Think of someone today who needs Gods forgiveness and ask for it.

MONDAY:

I tell you the truth, today you will be with Me in paradise.

Luke 23:43 (NKJV)

Jesus knew He was going to be in paradise this very day, and He wanted those around Him to join Him there if they so chose. Those who hung on crosses next to Jesus were definitely sinners. We cannot say they deserved the cross or even that they deserved to die, but they did deserve punishment. They were at their weakest moment on their crosses too. Jesus knew who and what they had done; yet His provision was mercy to the point of paradise. So even if you are in the midst of punishment, Jesus will provide the mercy needed for you to join Him in His paradise.

Is there sin in your life for which you have not asked forgiveness? Ask Him now; He will provide for you in a time of trial.

TUESDAY:

> He said to His mother, "Woman, behold your son!" Then He said to the disciple, "Behold your mother!"
>
> John 19:26b–27a (NKJV)

Jesus was and is today all about making provisions for you. The loss of someone we love often causes us to focus on the negatives. Jesus knew focusing on the negatives is not in our best interest. He provided an opportunity for His mother and His disciple to focus on something that would be a positive for both. They could respond to and for each other. If you have been handed a loss or know someone who has, provide a positive for him or her or yourself to focus on for a while.

What positive can come to light in the midst of the loss of a loved one?

WEDNESDAY:

> And about the ninth hour Jesus cried out with a loud voice, saying, "Eli, Eli, lama sabachthani?" that is, *"My God, My God, why have You forsaken Me?"*
>
> Matthew 27:46 (NKJV)

There was even a moment on the cross when Jesus felt forsaken by God. There must have been a time in your life when you felt forsaken in some manner. By this scripture we know Jesus knows exactly how we feel and will make a provision for you in the current trial you are going through. God is supremely holy and will never be in the midst of sin. Because Jesus took on all our sins, God had no choice but to turn His back on him. Jesus did what His Father requested, but He still had to bare the pain of our sins, which was separation from His Holy Father. When we have sinned, we are separated from our Holy Father. But because Jesus was forsaken on the cross, all we have to do is confess our sin, and we are again in God's presence.

Tell God how thankful you are His Son paid the price of sin and now there is a way for you to stay in His presence.

THURSDAY:

He said, "Father, into Your hands, I commit my spirit."

Luke 23:46b (NKJV)

Jesus made a commitment to His Father and to the world, and He kept it. Jesus so trusted His Father that even in His darkest moment, He remained committed to God's desires. We too must commit to our Father in all our circumstances and trust in His outcome.

Tell God and yourself today of your commitment.

FRIDAY:

> He said, "It is finished!" And bowing His head, He gave up His spirit.
>
> John 19:30b (NKJV)

Jesus had finished the work God gave Him to do on this earth. Now it was time to rejoin God in heaven. Jesus freely gave all, including His life for us. At the moment He gave up His spirit, He made it possible for you to spend eternity with Him. If you have not given your life and spirit to Jesus, do it today. Ask Him now to forgive your sins, and tell Him you trust Him to be your Savior and Lord. Amen. It too is finished for you.

If you are just now asking Jesus into your life, write how it makes you feel. If you have done this in the past, write how it made you feel then.

SATURDAY:

> He is not here, but is raised! Remember how He spoke to you when He was still in Galilee, saying, "The Son of Man must be delivered into the hands of sinful men, be crucified and on the third day be risen."
>
> Luke 24:6–7 (NKJV)

Jesus had told those who would listen He would rise again, and He did just what He said. This is our testament for the proof that He lives today. If Jesus had not been raised from the dead, all He told us would be for naught. It all would have been a lie. If the truth is not in His resurrection, then the truth is not in the Bible. The truth is: He did rise and is coming again.

Remind yourself today of the truth of His resurrection, that He lives today, and what that means to you now.

Prayer of Jabez

Autumn closes with December opening. It is a time of year we may wonder, "Where did the year go?" or "What did I do with *my* life this year?" With January approaching around the corner, do you start thinking about resolutions and how you can change yourself for the better? This week's daily devotions center on a man who is remembered for his prayer—a prayer some may think selfish. But if you are to better yourself, then don't you need to look at yourself? After all, it is yourself you are trying to change. And change will come if you dedicate yourselves to this type of prayer and you will be thrilled.

SUNDAY:

> And Jabez was more honourable than his brethren: and his mother called his name Jabez, saying, Because I bare him with sorrow.
>
> 1 Chronicles 4:9 (KJV)

Finding these two phrases together confused me until I prayed. My own view on this is that Jabez's mother had already born several "boys." Life was hard on her, and then Bam! She was pregnant again. Perhaps, it was a hard pregnancy, but the Bible uses the word "sorrow" not pain. Therefore, I believe she felt within herself something to the effect of, "Another child! Lord, you know my heart is heavy with my children now. How can I deal with yet another child?" But she did. And praise God because that child's name ended up in the bible in the mist of a lot of lineage detail where other names are left out. Do you wonder why? First phrase: "More honourable." You can look to God and go through whatever he lays before you, and know that God will be in control, if we allow it. If you are in sorrow today, give it over to God. He will make your sorrow yield results, 'More honourable.' What sorrows can you lay before him today?

MONDAY:

And Jabez called on the God of Israel, saying …

1 Chronicles 4:10a (KJV)

Did you pray the prayer of Jabez today? The recording of this awesome prayer begins with "And Jabez was more honourable than his brethren." I am sure he was not haughty or high-minded about this, because then he wouldn't really have been "honorable." You too can be honorable, and even *more* honorable. How? Do as Jabez and call on God. He will keep you honorable. There is a lot the word honorable encompasses, so check out your dictionary. I think you will be amazed. For now, call on God.

TUESDAY:

Oh that thou wouldest bless me indeed.

1 Chronicles 4:10b (KJV)

Here is Jabez, whose name means pain, coming right out and asking God to bless him. He goes a step farther and adds the indeed. I looked that word up. 'Indeed' actually goes back to a previous word used to give it 'more,' to give it 'strength,' or to add 'emphasis.' Think about this today. Jabez did not just ask for the Lord to bless him. He asked the Lord to *bless him and bless him indeed.* Again, my rendition, pour it on me Lord, not just a little, but really flood me with your blessing. You are *not* being selfish to ask God for His blessings. God wants to bless you. Ask Him today. "Oh that thou wouldest bless me indeed."

WEDNESDAY:

And enlarge my coast.

1 Chronicles 4:10b (KJV)

We have to go to a word study to get the meat of this request. Coast is not just a shoreline. My wonderful friend *Webster* also gives the word *frontier* as a definition for "coast." "It is a border between two countries, a stronghold—a region that forms the margin of settled or developed territory—the farthermost limits of knowledge or achievement in a particular subject."

Jabez asked for his "stronghold," his "margin" to be enlarged. Pray this prayer today:

Jesus, enlarge the territory that is settled within me. Allow the limits to stretch and grow. Make the line that divides the calm and the raging within me to move, and make way for more calm in my soul.

THURSDAY:

And that thine hand might be with me.

1 Chronicles 4:10b (KJV)

Jabez knew that in order for him to "live up to" this prayer request, he could *not* be the one in control. The control must come from God and God alone. I looked up the word *hand,* and in one simple definition, I found the reason for Jabez asking for God's *hand* to be with him. I went to the following site: www.wordnetweb.princetion.edu and found they define hand as:the (prehensile) extremity of the superior limb; In a more detailed, yet general site I found them to consider the hands to be principal organs for physically manipulating the environment. The fingertips have very dense nerve endings and give an intense feedback. This is God's hand that is with you, the hand that truly has the power to "manipulate" the environment. Praise Him today knowing *his hand* keeps you safe and secure.

FRIDAY:

> That thou wouldest keep me from evil, that it may not grieve me!
>
> 1 Chronicles 4:10b (KJV)

It may seem as if this is a selfish request, but consider the complete picture of this prayer. Jabez wanted to live for God, and he wanted to do a work for God. This may be one of the most powerful requests that can be made. Satan tries to slither into our lives in a very subtle way, which brings us ever so slightly into evil. Jabez had the exact right prayer. Being in evil (however slightly) does make a child of God grieve. You are not effective if you are grieving. You can become sad, despondent, and even depressed at your failure to stay away from evil. This is a prayer request that you *need.* What evil can you ask God to keep you from that it may not grieve you?

SATURDAY:

And God granted him that which he requested.

1 Chronicles 4:10b (KJV)

Have you ever been in a situation in which you needed (in your mind) an answer to your prayer, and you needed it *now* or "yesterday," if you know what I mean? Of course, we all have. We have needed, wanted, and even pined for our petition to be granted. Then we are told to wait … When you read this verse, notice that God does in fact grant the request, and you do not always have to wait. The key to remember is that God *granted* the request. Use the space below to thank God for providing strength and comfort while you wait.

Designing Us

Some of you may remember the TV show *Designing Women.* It came to mind a few days ago. The show was based on four women designing rooms for clients. In a sense, we are clients of God, and He is designing us to be the most beautiful Christian we can be. He works from the inside bringing His design to the outside. In the blueprint process, changes will be made, ones that will take you from the darkness of trials to the brightness of hope. This is the hope that Christ will put in your new design.

SUNDAY:

> So God created man in his own image, in the image of God he created him; male and female he created them."
>
> Genesis 1: 27 (NIV)

The verse today uses the word *created* three times. This must be important to know. Every design begins with the basics. God's foundation for us began with His image. Your beginning started with His likeness. Think of this today; and know that He created you in His image.

Write out one characteristic of God you want to have, and pray for God to help you be like Him.

MONDAY:

> For you created my inmost being; you knit me together in my mother's womb, I praise you because I am fearfully and wonderfully made ...
>
> Psalm 139:13–14a (NIV)

God created you in your mother's womb. He knew what he was creating before your earthly parents knew. Your mind, body, and soul were created in His image, fearfully and wonderfully. Do you see the design He is bringing about in you?

Use the lines below to thank Him for the magnificent you He is crafting.

TUESDAY:

> Before I formed you in the womb I knew you, before you were born I set you apart; I appointed you as a prophet to the nations.
>
> Jeremiah 1:5 (NIV)

God created you for a purpose. He knows you and set you apart to be His. To know His purpose for you, seek Him and His word. Take today, and spend time with Christ asking: "For what purpose has He set me apart?"

Write your prayer out below asking Him for what purpose you were created.

WEDNESDAY:

> From one man he made every nation of men, that they should inhabit the whole earth; and he determined the times set for them and the exact places where they should live.
>
> Acts 17:26 (NIV)

God determined your time and your place. Today may be a day a trial has hit you with not knowing where or what. He has given you the tools needed to go through this trial. No matter today's situation, what will you do with what He has given you?

Think on the tools He has given you to make it through any trial you have already gone through. Write them below, and if they are needed again, then pick them up. They still work.

THURSDAY:

> Yet, O LORD, you are our Father. We are the clay, you are the potter; we are all the work of your hand."
>
> Isaiah 64:8 (NIV)

We are the work of God's hands. Do you see cracks in the structure He is making of you? He continues to form you until He is finished making the perfect work of His hands. Today, allow Him to work you, as a potter works the clay.

What are the cracks you see in yourself, write them out below. Then write how He has perfected those cracks to make a better you.

FRIDAY:

> But the pot he was shaping from the clay was marred in his hands; so the potter formed it into another pot, shaping it as seemed best to him."
>
> Jeremiah 18:4 (NIV)

God knows the design He has set for you. He desires to shape you into that design. Have the trials of your life seemed to mold you into something different than what you intended? The trials in your life may be part of the design. Ask and know how He would have you use these trials. Spend time today with Him, so you may become His design.

Use the lines below to ask and know how He would have you to use those trials.

SATURDAY:

> Neither do men pour new wine into old wineskins. If they do, the skins will burst, the wine will run out and the wineskins will be ruined. No, they pour new wine into new wineskins, and both are preserved."
>
> Matthews 9:17 (NIV)

Each day is a new day. Continuing in your old habits is like putting new wine into old wineskins. You are sure to burst! Don't allow the new wine back in the old skin. Spend time with God every day to become new wine in a new wineskin.

List those old habits you want to put away so you will not burst. Thank God for the new wine skin He is giving you.

His Teaching Continues

One of Gods greatest provisions for us in times of trials is the teachings of Jesus both when He walked here on earth and after He arose. Though His physical body was gone Jesus still had much to teach us.

SUNDAY:

> Now when evening had come, there came a rich man from Arimathea, named Joseph, who himself had also become a disciple of Jesus. This man went to Pilate and asked for the body of Jesus. Then Pilate commanded the body to be given to him. When Joseph had taken the body, he wrapped it in a clean linen cloth and laid it in the new tomb which he had hewn out of the rock; and he rolled a large stone against the door of the tomb and departed.
>
> Matthew 27:57–60 (NKJV)

God's provisions for us are never ending, just as they were for Jesus. His physical body had taken all the punishment it could withstand. The time had passed for His physical body to be of use. But God still had work for Jesus to do in the way of witnessing to all. No matter your circumstance, God intends for you to be a witness for Him.

To whom might you be a witness today?

MONDAY:

> But the angel answered and said to the women, "Do not be afraid, for I know that you seek Jesus who was crucified. He is not here; for He is risen, as He said. Come, see the place where the Lord lay."
>
> Matthew 28: 5–6 (NKJV)

Sometimes we are naturally aware of God's miracles. Then there are times we must be shown these miracles, so we know exactly what God has provided. Open your heart today. Ask God to take you to His place and to let you see what He has laid for you.

At the end of today, write what God showed you in the way of miracles.

TUESDAY:

> Then the same day at evening, being the first day of the week, when the doors were shut where the disciples were assembled, for fear of the Jews, Jesus came and stood in the midst, and said to them, "Peace be with you."
>
> John 20:19 (NKJV)

Jesus always comes to us in peace. Our circumstances may have left us in fear, weariness, or indecision. The darkness or light in your day does not matter call to Him! He will approach with love, peace, and understanding.

Remind yourself of a time you were in fear or just weary and you called to Jesus.

WEDNESDAY:

> So Jesus said to them again, "Peace to you! As the Father has sent Me, I also send you."
>
> John 20:21 (NKJV)

When Jesus spoke these words, He had just shown the disciples the scars left by His crucifixion, not to bring trembling and fear, but to get their attention, so they would know who was standing in their presence. It was important for Him to tell the disciples one more time of the plans He had for them. He fully understood their hiding out, but it was important for them to remember what all the past three years had really been about. The same is true for today! He knows where you are, and He wants to send you out!

Where can you go today for Jesus and make a difference?

THURSDAY:

> Jesus said to him, "Thomas because you have seen Me, you have believed. Blessed are those who have not seen and yet have believed."
>
> John 20:29 (NKJV)

We cannot see, nor have we seen, Jesus in His physical body. But we can see His works. He offers you special blessings, because you continue to love and serve Him without being able to touch Him physically as Thomas required.

How might your faith be different if you could have physically touched Jesus?

FRIDAY:

> And when He had said this, He breathed on them and said to them, "Receive the Holy Spirit, If you forgive the sins of any, they are forgiven them; if you retain the sins of any, they are retained."
>
> John 20:22–23 (NKJV)

Here, Jesus tries to emphasize to the disciples, the responsibilities of their position. If we call ourselves Christians, we have the same responsibilities today. If we cannot forgive, have we set in motion an event that we cannot control? Allowing our hearts to harden, because of a hurt can cause just such an event! Look into your heart today, and see if forgiveness needs to be given.

Have you retained a sin against you in your heart? Write to Jesus about it today.

SATURDAY:

> And being assembled together with them, He commanded them not to depart from Jerusalem, but to wait for the Promise of the Father, "which," He said, "you have heard from Me; for John truly baptized with water, but you shall be baptized with the Holy spirit not many days from now."
>
> Acts 1:4–5 (NKJV)

More than anything, it is important we are where Jesus wants us to be when He wants us to be there. We may be confused at His timing or His place. Our reliance on His judgments for perfection is what He is asking. He will provide all that is needed, no matter where we are at the moment.

Where does Jesus want you to be this day, this moment? Are you doing everything you can to follow Him? He has provided the way.

The Beginning

Beginnings have trials all their own. But God has made provisions for those trials too. When we are in a new year, we see ourselves at a new beginning. With that in mind, the devotions this week will be on Genesis 1. It was a time of beginning. We will look at how God began our world and how we can use this knowledge to focus our new beginning.

SUNDAY:

> In the beginning God created the heavens and the earth. Now the earth was formless and empty.
>
> Genesis 1: 1–2a (NKJV)

God began by taking nothing and creating this world and His heavens. As we begin this week, let's first praise Him for what He has done. Next, let's meditate on how there was nothing, then there was something—His creation. This something was not just anything … it was the world! If He can do this, then surely He can take the nothings that we believe we have and create them into something. Spend time with Him today telling Him about your nothings and asking Him to create them into the something He can use.

What trials might you see ahead because nothing has now become something?

MONDAY:

God said, "Let there be light," and there was light.

Genesis 1:3 (NKJV)

Do you feel you are walking in darkness and cannot or do not know where your next step should be? Call upon your Father. He is the creator of light. He will bring the light into focus for you. He will light your path and show you where your foot is to step. He created the light, and He is the light to follow. Today, call upon Him to light your path.

What darkness do you face today that He can light up for you?

TUESDAY:

> And God said, "Let there be an expanse between the waters to separate water from water." So God made the expanse and separated the water under the expanse from the water above it. And it was so. God called the expanse "sky," and there was evening and there was morning... the second day.
>
> Genesis 1:6–8 (NKJV)

Sometimes we wake up from a sleep and say, "Oh, another morning to go and do all that I must do." Instead of doing that, today let's begin by praising Him for the day He has given us. He knows all that will come and go. Allow Him to show you this day and invite Him to be a part of your day.

Write your request.

WEDNESDAY:

> Then God said, "Let the land produce vegetation; seed-bearing plants and trees on the land that bear fruit with seed in it, according to their various kinds," and it was so."
>
> Genesis 1:11 (NKJV)

Vegetation, plants, and trees—they are beautiful to look at, and they also provide for us. They delight our eyes and our stomachs. Only a God like ours could have created something that would delight us in many ways. As you go on your way to work or even just step outside your door today, praise Him for what He has given. He is feeding us with nutrition to our brains and bodies. Thank Him today, all day long.

THURSDAY:

> God made two great lights—the greater light to govern the day and the lesser light to govern the night. He also made the stars. God set them in the expanse of the sky to give light on the earth, to govern the day and the night, and to separate light from darkness."
>
> Genesis 1:16–18a (NKJV)

God is still giving us light to show us the way. The light of the day brings us warmth. The warmth comforts us when we are cold or feeling down. A sunny day can lift our spirits, sometimes when nothing else can. The moon and stars at night can be so relaxing after a long day. We can gaze upon them and know The One who put them there. Take this day to mediate on all He did when He created the sun, the moon, and the stars.

Tell yourself now what the day light means to you and what the night stars show you.

FRIDAY:

> So God created the great creatures of the sea and every living and moving thing with which the water teems, and according to their kinds, and every winged bird according to its kind … God blessed them …
>
> Genesis 1:21–22a (NKJV)

God created the birds, the fish, and all the animals of this world. Then He blessed them. He thinks enough of these creations to bless them. The knowledge of His blessings helps us realize what a gracious God we have. If you are having a trial with food issues, remember the blessings God bestowed. Look to Him to know when to eat and how much to eat at each setting. Praise Him today for His blessings.

Ask for His grace toward all your trials no matter what they may be.

SATURDAY:

> Then God said, "Let us make man in our image, in our likeness"… So God created man in his own image, in the image of God he created him; male and female he created them."
>
> Genesis 1:26a–27 (NKJV)

To make something is to assemble something, but to create means to bring something into existence. God created you and me. He brought us into existence and made us into beings. Today ask God what He means for you to be. You are His, so allow Him to make you into the one He desires for you to be.

Will there be changes to you if you ask Him to make you to His liking? If so, what will those changes be?

Freedom From the Laws of Sin

Ever hear someone say, "I'd become a Christian, but there are just too many rules?" This is one of Satan's biggest lies and often used in today's society. Changing from a non-Christian to a Christian does have its trials and tribulations, but God is there with His provisions. People today talk incessantly about "their freedoms" and all the encroachments being put upon those freedoms. Laws and rules are given for protection and guidance. Satan takes truth and freedom and turns them into lies and captivity.

Here are at least seven truths from God. Because we belong to him and have chosen to follow Jesus Christ, we gain these freedoms and more:

SUNDAY:

> There is therefore now no condemnation to those who are in Christ Jesus, who do not walk according to the flesh, but according to the Spirit.
>
> Romans 8:1 (NKJV)

The scripture tells us if we are leading our lives to follow Jesus Christ, we cannot be condemned. It doesn't say "maybe" we will make it to righteousness. It says "now *no* condemnation." Does this mean we will never make mistakes? *No!* Jesus Christ died on the cross for all our sins. So when we give ourselves over to *him,* we cannot be condemned. This includes the sins of yesterday, today, and tomorrow.

How does it make you feel to know you are not condemned?

MONDAY:

> For to be carnally minded is death, but to be spiritually minded is life and peace.
>
> Romans 8:6 (NKJV)

To be carnally minded is to be thinking and doing as the world sees fit. As in the days of Noah, everyone was doing what was right in their own eyes (Matthew 24:38). Being spiritually minded is following the ways of Jesus Christ. Learning the ways of the Holy Spirit, we become spiritually minded, and we are given life and peace—a peace our non-Christian friends cannot claim. When was the last time you could say one of those friends had true peace? Take a moment, and pray for them today.

Put your prayer in writing.

TUESDAY:

> But you are not in the flesh but in the Spirit, if indeed the Spirit of God dwells in you. Now if anyone does not have the Spirit of Christ, he is not His.
>
> Romans 8:9 (NKJV)

If the Spirit of God is in you, you will think and act like Jesus Christ. If you do not have the Spirit of Christ, you do not belong to Him. We demonstrate we possess the Spirit or live in the flesh every time we speak or act. If you are unsure you posses the Spirit, ask God. Ask His forgiveness for your sins. Tell him of your trust in Jesus Christ. Allow Him to lead, guide, and direct every aspect of your life from this moment forward.

Which spririt fills you today? How do you know?

WEDNESDAY:

> And if Christ is in you, the body is dead because of sin, but the Spirit is life because of righteousness."
>
> Romans 8:10 (NKJV)

If you belong to Christ, though your body may die, your spirit will have life. Because Jesus died on the cross and rose again, you can have a Spirit of righteousness. This is God's promise. Claiming God's promise by accepting Jesus as your personal Savior gives you the Spirit of righteousness.

If you have never trusted in Christ, do it today. If you have accepted Him as your personal Savior, pray for someone you know who has not.

THURSDAY:

> For as many as are led by the Spirit of God, these are sons of God.
>
> Romans 8:14 (NKJV)

If we have received salvation and are led by the Spirit we are now called sons of God. There are no additional "rules" to follow. There are no additional strings attached. So when you hear someone say, "I'd become a Christian, but there are too many rules," you can now respond by claiming your freedoms: no condemnations, no contentions, and no carnal mind—you are *free.*

Write how you will respond to someone stating the "becoming a Christian but" statement. This way you will be ready to respond.

FRIDAY:

> For you did not receive the spirit of bondage again to fear, but you received the Spirit of adoption, by whom we cry out, "Abba, Father."
>
> Romans 8:15 (NKJV)

Once we have accepted Christ Jesus as our Savior and Lord, we have given up any bondage. We have also been given freedom from fear. As children, we look to our parent(s) in fearful situations. By receiving the Spirit of adoption, we can now call upon our Holy Father in all circumstances. Cry out to your "Abba Father," and let Him be in control.

Tell Him some of your fears today.

SATURDAY:

> Likewise the Spirit also helps in our weaknesses. For we do not know what we should pray for as we ought, but the Spirit Himself makes intercession for us with groanings which cannot be uttered.
>
> Romans 8:26 (NKJV)

We can now confidentially say as Christians, we do not have a set of earthly rules to follow. In addition, even at our weakest points, we can ask our Father for his care. If we are unsure or cannot find the words to use, the Holy Spirit will step in with utterances we cannot understand and intercede to the Father. Ask your non-Christian friends which column below, they might choose:

FREEDOM	LAWS OF SIN
Follow Christ	Follow the World
Life	Death
Righteousness	Sin
Let all be in God's control	Try to take control
Let the Spirit plead our cause	Work it out as best we can

There is definitely a choice to be made. It seems like an easy choice, but maybe not …

PART IV

winter

YOU ARE NOT LEFT OUT IN THE COLD BY YOUR SAVIOR.

WINTER

There is a veil upon me;
It feels wet and cold.
I want to feel easy and free,
But instead the veil
Has too tight a hold.

This breeze began soft and low;
Now the stroke is so severe.
I begin to hear my Father;
He calls me, "One so dear."

The Words He speaks
Gently upon me rest.
I am comforted to know
My future He has filled
With only His best.

—Kathleen J. Jones—

Winter can bring ice storms, blizzards, and cold rain. Step into these pages, and enjoy a crisp new day filled with God's *peace, love,* and *joy.* These scriptures and devotions will give you *hope* and fill your soul with *love* from the Father above.

If

If? This small little word can plague our hearts and minds. It is a little word, but it packs a big punch. We can dwell on our lives wondering things like: "What if I had done …, "What if I changed …" "What if I did not …" or "If only …" Wondering and dwelling on these questions will not give us the answers. This week, that little word "if" will show you hope, love, and bring us to the Christ that answered these questions for all mankind.

SUNDAY:

> If it had not been the LORD who was on our side, now may Israel say; If it had not been the LORD who was on our side, when men rose up against us.
>
> Psalm 124:1–2 (KJV)

Like it or not, we are on a side. When all is said and done, there are only two sides. Both sides answer to the True and Living God. Whatever you are going through today, you can win if the LORD is on your side. Read and pray these verses today. You have strength in *Him.*

MONDAY:

> If thou wilt do this thing, and GOD command thee so, then thou shalt be able to endure.
>
> Exodus 18:23 (KJV)

Our lives are full of choices. Those choices bring consequences and a variety of results.

Exodus 18:23 tells us if we but do as God commands, we can endure. When you listen to your own commands, you yield zero endurance. If you can do as He commands, you *will* endure. Ponder on that today.

TUESDAY:

> And it shall be, if thou will hearken to all that I command thee ... that I will be with thee, and build thee a sure house.
>
> 1 Kings 11:38 (KJV)

Listening to God's commands not only allows you to endure as you learned yesterday, but also, you can now see that God will be with you and will build you a sure house. Read His Word and know when everything seems to be crumbling around you, your foundation is sure for He is your hope.

WEDNESDAY:

> Then Jesus said unto his disciples,"If any man will come after me let him deny himself, and take up his cross, and follow me."
>
> Matthew 16:24 (KJV)

Today's society speaks of the lack of equality. I wonder at times what equality is, and if is it real. God's Word shows us in this verse that according to God *any*one can come to Him. You do not have to pass a test, be a certain race, or even have a specific social level. We are all equal in His eyes. We have only to deny ourselves, take up our crosses, and follow Jesus. Consider the various ways you can follow Jesus. Step in his footprints when you walk out in the cold and snow.

THURSDAY:

Beloved, if God so loved us, we ought to love one another.

1 John 4:11 (KJV)

While driving down the highway or shopping in a store, it is rare to see the love of God in or coming from our fellow man. It is hard to put this verse into our everyday lives when others are not kind to us. We become filled with negative emotions and respond to others in a like manner. But we are not told to treat others as they treat us. We are told to love one another. Dig deep within yourself today, and show the love of God is abundant and alive. Let his love warm others through your obedience.

FRIDAY:

If any man hath an ear, let him hear.

Revelation 13:9 (KJV)

Have you ever talked to someone and felt they weren't really listening? Maybe they seemed to be in another zone and not focusing on the conversation. God says if you have an ear, then hear. Focus upon Jesus and listen intently to His conversation. Everyone is invited to hear Him. Are you listening to God? Pray for open ears. The choice to hear is yours.

SATURDAY:

> If thou shalt confess with thy mouth the Lord Jesus, and shalt believe in thine heart that God hath raised Him from the dead, thou shalt be saved.
>
> Romans 10:9 (KJV)

Friday, we ended with "the choice is yours." Today's verse reveals that Christ is the only answer to the "if" question. Receive the "if" answer today. Maybe, you are already a child of God? If so, go out, and help others receive the answer of "if," and come to Christ today. "If" you will, they can.

Micah

A cold and dreary time can be felt regardless of the actual climatic season. One of my most vivid times of dispear from my memory is actually during the end of summer. I was sending my eldest child off for his first time. I was in the military, and as I stood outside the door, tears filled my eyes and overflowed down my cheeks. An officer walked by, and I struggled to salute. He was gracious and must have understood or at least felt compassion for a very young mother, because he gave the "at ease" quickly and made conversation, which "eased" my aching heart.

Take time to read each chapter in Micah this week. I pray you too will see a God that feels compassion and gives us the "at ease." He will show through His Word that you have a *choice* in how you live your life.

SUNDAY:

> The word of the LORD that came to Micah … concerning Samaria and Jerusalem … "Make thee bald, enlarge thy baldness as the eagle."
>
> Micah 1:1, 16 (KJV)

You can be sure when the word of the LORD comes concerning your sin, you will receive judgment. This chapter tells of the transgression and sins of the house of Samaria and Jerusalem and shows that *He* discovered their foundation. Evil and transgression was found. We are told to enlarge our baldness (if someone is bald they can not hide anything on their head—we see all). Open up to God today. Reveal your transgressions to Him.

MONDAY:

Woe to them that devise iniquity … this time is evil.

Micah 2:1 (KJV)

Today's chapter is a hard one to grasp. The world we live in today is evil. Think about the crime alone. Those commiting crimes are planning and formulating a way to get what they desire. I chose this verse, because we have a responsibility as Christians to show the love of Christ to an evil world. Ask God to tell you how to show His love today. Others are out in the harsh and cold times. Take time to plan and formulate a way to show others the love of Jesus.

TUESDAY:

They shall all cover their lips; for there is no answer of God.

Micah 3:7b (KJV)

Have you ever been so shocked that your mouth dropped open, and you covered your lips? I have, and it is usually not a 'good' shock. God knows your every deed. But will he cover his mouth in distress? How can you live for him today?

WEDNESDAY:

He will teach us his ways, and we will walk in His paths.

Micah 4:2b (KJV)

It is midweek, and what a great day to read this chapter and know that the Lord will redeem us from the hand of our enemies. Even though the trials of life bring pain "as a woman in childbirth," you can gather together to "Arise and thresh."

THURSDAY:

Such as they have not heard.

Micah 5:15b (KJV)

This week's subject is the compassion of God and the hope that you have in him. In this chapter, we learn God is on target and is preparing to take action. The false prophets and soothsayers mentioned here should have been concerned, but sadly they probably were not then and some people are not today. God is in protection mode for those of us that have agreed to "walk in his paths." If you have not agreed to "walk in his paths," won't you do that now? Write your thoughts regarding any concerns you have.

FRIDAY:

O my people, what have I done unto thee?

Micah 6:3 (KJV)

As a mother, I can just feel God's painful heart. When my child acted unruly, it wounded my heart. I had to ask my child, "Why? What have I done to you that would make you go against my rules? Breaking the rules does not leave you feeling full or satisfied." Sin does not satisfy. God's love and compassion is the only true satisfaction. Confess the wrongs you have done to God, accept his forgivness, and move forward out of the harsh weather.

SATURDAY:

> He will turn again, he will have compassion upon us; he will subdue our iniquities; and thou wilt cast all their sins into the depths of the sea.
>
> Micah 7:19 (KJV)

The reality of God's compassion is upon us. Through the entire book of Micah, we have seen God's children listen to the "wrong crowd." Then they returned to the God of compassion. It is true that God will have compassion upon you, and He will subdue your iniquities ... you must simpy ask in Jesus name. Show others the compassion of Christ. Be a witness today.

Senses

Have you ever thought about your senses being in the Bible? Well, why not? After all, God did give them to you? You use your senses everyday in whatever you are doing. Do you ever think about how you use them for God's purposes? It is said there are only five senses, but to finish the week, let's consider an extra two: knowing and admitting. This week discover using your senses through Him and how God works them so you will know He is always there.

SUNDAY:

The Lord gives sight to the blind.

Psalm 146:8 (NIV)

How many times are you blinded by what you do not want to see? You know the truth, but deep down, you do not want to admit it. Focus on His truth today; on the signifance of God being truth and how He sets you free from bondage. He will never leave you in a darkness of lies. Let *His light* shine, so you may fully focus on Him.

Tell Him of the darkness in you He has brought to the light. Thank in for being your light. Use the area below to write out your thankfulness.

MONDAY:

> Blessed are those who hear it and take to heart what is written.
>
> Revelation 1:3 (NIV)

Sometimes when you hear something someone has told you was from God do you wonder, "Is that really what God meant?" Just listening to others speak His word is not the only way to know His truth. He can fill your heart by what others speak, but He will also fill your heart directly. Pray and ask for His understandings as you read His word today.

Write out your prayer as you ask for understanding of His word.

TUESDAY:

Taste and see that the Lord is good.

Psalm 34:8 (NIV)

Does just thinking about your favorite food give your mouth a good feeling? The Lord is just like that favorite food, only better. Daily tasting what He has to say is better than any food you could ever put to your tongue. This day may not be one of the best chunks of your favorite food, but the Lord will add a topping you cannot resist. Just give this day to Him for the frosting.

Thank Him for the wonderful flavors He is going to give you today. Use the lines below to name some of your favorite taste and how He could bring those to life in your day. Example: He takes the pits out of the cherries or dipping strawberries into chocolate gives a sweeter taste to the day.

WEDNESDAY:

For we are to God the aroma of Christ.

2 Corinthians 2:15 (NIV)

When you light candles then walk out of the room; do you come back in to smell the sweet aroma? In God's Word today you are the aroma of Christ to God. What better smell can there be than Christ? He is here for you daily, so that you may take in the wonderous smell of your Savior. Today, thank the Lord for dying on the cross, so you could be the aroma of Him to your Father in heaven.

Smell the sweet aroma of Christ in you. Write out your prayer of thanks below.

THURSDAY:

She thought, "If I could just touch his cloak."

Mark 5:28 (NIV)

This woman knew that she could be healed by just touching Christ's garment. What faith! Do you ever think about what it would have been like to touch His garment? We cannot physically touch His cloak, but we can touch His Word to know Him. We can know Him through prayer and study. He will touch your heart and heal you.

Tell Him how He has touched your heart and healed you by His Word. Write out your prayer of thanks to Him.

FRIDAY:

For all have sinned and fall short of the glory of God.

Romans 3:23 (NIV)

Knowing is not a real sense but in knowing you can begin to understand how you use many of your senses to commit sin. Touch, taste and see the things you shouldn't. Sin is part of you as a human being. You can use those same senses to stop your sinfulness, by stop touching, tasting and seeing the things of the evil one. You cannot be perfect, but you do know the One who is. Ask for His forgiveness, and use your senses for His glory.

Write out your prayer asking for forgiveness; ask how you can use your senses for His glory.

SATURDAY:

Having been justified by his grace, we should become heirs.

Titus 3:7 (NIV)

You are justified by His grace. You are a sinner, but you are a forgiven sinner. God gave His Son, so you would have grace. His grace allows you to be an heir in the kingdom of God. This grace permits you to be a sibling of Christ. Praise your Father. He has given you what no one else could or ever will be able to give you.

Describe your appreciation for His grace and what it means in your life below.

Phrases We Often Use

There are times we feel all alone, left out, or in times of despair; there are common phrases we tend to dwell in and on. They are expressions we think on because we are in a desparate place. We want to be loved and accepted but feel left out in the cold. This week we will focus on some of those sayings and bring them to the light of God. Bring them out into the open for God to show us they are lies and He is not the Father of lies. For in seeking Him, the truth will come out into the open, and we will see His light in our darkness.

SUNDAY:

> Jesus replied, "What is impossible with men is possible with God."
>
> Luke 18:27 (NIV)

We say, "It is impossible." Try as you might, even with hundreds assisting, sometimes you just cannot get "it" done. The scripture says you are right. It may be impossible for man, but if God is involved, it is possible. You need to have just the right people to get a job done. Asking God is always the "right people." Put your trust in Him, and He will make it possible.

Let Him know how He is the 'right people' for you. Write it out as if it was a letter of recommendation telling of the excellent job He has done for you.

MONDAY:

> For God so loved the world that he gave his one and only Son, that whoever believes in him shall not perish but have eternal life.
>
> John 3:16 (NIV)

You may have said or felt like there were times when nobody really loved you. But there is one who knows what love is and loves you every moment of the day. Do you know if you were the only person on this earth, Christ would still have died on the cross for you? You may not have a spouse, boyfriend, or even a really good friend whom you feel loves you enough, especially if they knew everything about you. But God knew about you before you were born, and He still sent His Son to die on the cross for you. You are really loved.

Use the lines below to tell Him of your need for His love. Read back the words after writing them and you will hear Him saying them to you.

T U E S D A Y :

> Because God has said, "Never will I leave you; never will I forsake you."
>
> Hebrews 13:5b (NIV)

When you feel alone, you can remember His Word says He will never leave you. Therefore, you are never alone. You always have Him to go to with your prayers. The word *forsake* means to abandon or to give up. Your earthly loved ones may give up on or abandon you, but He never will. Even if you try to walk away from Him, He will continue to be there for you.

Do you have someone you feel left you? Use the area below to tell your Father about the feeling of being forsaken by them. Then tell Him of your thankfulness that He has never left you.

WEDNESDAY:

> For this reason, since the day we heard about you, we have not stopped praying for you and asking God to fill you with the knowledge of His will, through spiritual wisdom and understanding.
>
> Colossians 1:9 (NIV)

"I am not smart," you might say to yourself. But His Word tells you He will fill you with knowledge, wisdom, and understanding. This wisdom is not the wisdom as the world defines wisdom. It is His wisdom and His understanding. His wisdom and understanding comes from the beginning of time—something the world does not have. You become wise in Him and His ways when you spend time with Him in prayer and reading His Word. This makes you so much more than "smart."

Write out your prayer asking for His wisdom to understand His ways. Ask for His knowledge to comprehend how He doesn't leave you left out in the cold.

THURSDAY:

For God did not give us a spirit of timidity, but a spirit of power, of love and of self-discipline.

2 Timothy 1:17 (NIV)

Do you ever feel afraid? God gives you the power to *not* be afraid. He says, "I give you a spirit of power." Jesus left you with the Holy Spirit. It is that Spirit that allows you to not be afraid, to love with the agape love, and even to discipline yourself for His work. Call on the Holy Spirit in times when you feel fear, He is within you to help you through those times.

Name those fears on the lines below. Give them over to the Holy Spirit so you can be filled with His power.

FRIDAY:

> My grace is sufficient for you, for my power is made perfect in weakness.
>
> 2 Corinthians 12:9 (NIV)

When you feel weak and think you cannot go on, you can put your trust in Him. Hardships of this world can make you feel this kind of weakness. You must allow Him to help you when you are down. Your weaknesses are made perfect in His power. Even if you hold power in your grasp or hold a powerful position, it is not perfect power. You can go on, even in your weakest moments, because the perfection of His power is more than sufficient.

List where you feel you are weak. Now list the power God has given you to face those weaknesses. He gives you hope in His power.

SATURDAY:

> Trust in the Lord with all your heart and lean not on your own understanding; in all your ways acknowledge Him, and He will make your paths straight."
>
> Proverbs 3:5–6 (NIV)

When you feel confused and cannot figure things out, scripture tells you that is exactly where the Lord wants you. You are to lean on His understandings, and He will guide you, walk with you, and make the crooked ways become straight for you. When you are not sure what path to take, you can call on Him and acknowledge who He is. He will straighten your path and take away any confusion you might be experiencing.

What are you feeling confused about today? Write it out below; ask God to give you understanding of His ways.

Is It Worth It?

In the struggle through the wilderness the children of Israel murmured, "Would to God we would have stayed in Egypt" (as captives and not free). They were promised a land flowing with milk and honey. Yet they could not focus on the promise of God. They were told the outcome and chose to murmur and to complain instead of enjoying the fact that "*one day*" they would reap the benefits; their suffering would be worth it! What about us? We have been told the outcome. Are our present struggles worth it?

Just because we know the outcome does not mean getting there won't hurt. What we go through is nothing compared to the pain God felt on the day His Son died. God knew Jesus would be raised from the dead, yet He (God) had to turn his back on His very own Son and let Him suffer. God hurt for Jesus when Jesus died on the cross. God also knew by Jesus' death, we could have redemption and live eternally with Him.

SUNDAY:

> And the Egyptians made the children of Israel to serve with rigour; And they made their lives bitter with hard bondage.
>
> Exodus 1:13–14a (KJV)

You can become a slave in your own lfe without realizing you are falling into captivity. Imprisonment takes place one choice at a time, and pretty soon making choices without seeking your Father becomes a way of life. And so there you are–a slave. Choose to seek your Father in heaven in every aspect of your life.

MONDAY:

And God heard their groaning, and God remembered his covenant with Abraham, with Isaac, and with Jacob."

Exodus 2:24a (KJV)

Agreements today are broken as quickly as they are made but not so with God! A promise is sure when it is given by God. Even in the people's groaning, He remembered and acted on His promises. In your groaning, He hears you too. Be confident today and every day that God will remember and will take action. The promises from so long ago are yours still. Trust Him to hear you.

TUESDAY:

Rise up and get ye forth … and go, serve the Lord.

Exodus 12:31 (KJV)

Trials come and go. However, there are times you must live in your choices. No matter the situations, you can look at this verse, grab your boot straps, and then rise up, and go! It is hard; I know first-hand. Trust me, your relationship with Christ will be so amazing you will forget the pain you felt. So, come on, let's get *up* and *go.* Serve the Lord with gladness.

WEDNESDAY:

> And the children of Israel went into the midst of the sea upon the dry ground.
>
> Exodus 14:22 (KJV)

I am sure the Israelites were scared and tired, and their emotions were rolling. Yet in this impossible situation, God made a way for them, and He dried up the ground! No mud holes to sink into and slow them down. He will do this for you also. Consider the "Red Seas" you must cross. If you seek Him before you step into that water, he will dry the "land" for your safe passage. Pray over the seas you need a dry passge through.

THURSDAY:

> But now our soul is dried away: there is nothing at all, besides this manna, before our eyes.
>
> Numbers 11:6 (KJV)

We encourage you to take some time to read Exodus 15 through Numbers 12. It is a lot of reading, but you will enjoy learning of God's provision. Wait until you have time to relax and absorb the story. God's people were a long time in the wilderness! A lot happened there—the good with the bad—obedience and disobedience. But God always provided the peoples' needs. The problem was they wanted Him to provide their "wants." God had a lot for them to learn and knew they needed time. Some lessons take longer to learn than others, but throughout your "wilderness," God will provide for you.

FRIDAY:

> And they returned from searching of the new land after forty days.
>
> Numbers 13:25 (KJV)

Finally, it was time for the Israelites to come to their new land. They had been in the wilderness so long, they thought they would all die and never reach the Promised Land. So some disobeyed to the limit that they did not enjoy the bounty. How many times did the Israelites wonder, "Is there ever going to be any release?" God directed them right to the Promised Land. He continued to let them choose their course. This is so important for you to see. While Satan clouds your judgment in a way that you are confused to the max, God will gently guide and let you be the final decision maker. Satan does not do that. He will set the decision in such confusion and "pretty words" that you rush to make your choices. Let God direct you. Allow Him to lead you to the new land. He will let you "spy it out" before you dwell there. That is the beauty of an intimate relationship with God—you will be able to know the right thing to do!

SATURDAY:

> And Caleb stilled the people before Moses, and said "Let us go up at once, and possess it; for we are well able to overcome it."
>
> Numbers 13:30 (KJV)

Our devotion title this week is "Is it worth it?" Looking back on an extremely trying situation and knowing the splendor and awe of the outcome, the question comes to us: Was it worth it? Before we see the end result, we often ask ourselves, "Is it worth it?" Caleb saw the magnificence of this new land. He was assured and confident in the Lord and told the people they were *well able to overcome* the trials and tribulations they faced. It was all worth it to him. The trials and tribulations you go through may seem to be a horrid wilderness while you are in the midst of them, but if you can be *one that believes,* you too can look the situation in the face—eye to eye—and report, " I can go up *at once,* and possess it, for *I am well able to overcome it!*" A more intimate relationship with Christ is absolutely worth it. Believe today and every day!

Defining You

Did you know that even in the despondent times God is defining you? To define is to make clear, identify, or to explain. In times you are feeling downhearted; you can know Christ is making clear how you are His. You are His creation, as an individual, seeking and trusting Him to define you. Fix your eyes on His words to know who you are in Him.

SUNDAY:

> So God created man in his own image, in the image of God he created him male and female, He created them.
>
> Genesis 1:27 (NIV)

You were created by God not just something that came along. You were created to be someone special. Because you have been created in God's image that alone makes you special. In your time of testing, you have been created to examine His ways. Study His Word for you to know He is with you in this time. Go to Him for His explanation.

Use the lines below asking Him to show you how you are His creation and what you have been created to be as His child.

MONDAY:

> My frame was not hidden from "You" when I was made in the secret place.
>
> Psalm 139:15 (NIV)

When God created you, you were individually made. This means you are not from a cookie cutter. He alone made you precisely to His measurements for His work. For what work has He made you?

Write out your prayer below asking Him to reveal for what work He has made you.

TUESDAY:

> So I say to you; "ask and it will be given to you; seek and you will find; knock and the door will be opened to you."
>
> Luke 11:9 (NIV)

You are to seek Him in all ways. Seek to know Him more by reading His word, by praying to Him, and by worshiping Him all throughout the day. Discover the individual He made in you, His child, His friend and loved one.

Use the area below to seek and know Him. Think of the ways He has shown you He is your friend, you are His child, and loved one.

WEDNESDAY:

> Trust in the Lord with all your heart and lean not on your own understanding.
>
> Proverbs 3:5 (NIV)

To trust is to have confidence in the one you are trusting. He created you, you can rely on who He is and what He says and does. Trusting Him with your day means your trust grows for Him as does your love. Allow your love and understanding of His ways to grow in you.

Tell Him of your trust or you fear in trusting. List what it is that stops you from completely trusting in Him.

THURSDAY:

> My comfort in my suffering is this; Your promise preserves my life.
>
> Psalm 119:50 (NIV)

You are assured by His promise to be with Him in eternity. That promise will strengthen you as you endure life's daily bumps. When you suffer and need His assurances, call on your Savior for His promise. He is listening and waiting to hear from you. Go ahead call—on Him today.

Use the area below to write out your prayer of calling to Him. Thank Him for His promises, and gain strength from His assurances.

FRIDAY:

> The path of the righteous is like the first glean of dawn shining ever brighter till the full light of day.
>
> Proverbs 4:18 (NIV)

You were made righteous the moment you asked Him to be your Lord. It is through Him your righteousness will shine like the first of the dawn. Your righteousness will grow ever brighter with each day. Learn from Him, and let His light shine through you so that you will light the way for others to see Him.

Today ask Him to show you how you can allow His righteousness to grow in you that you may show others. Use the space below to write it out.

SATURDAY:

> Say to wisdom, "You are my sister," and call understanding your kinsman.
>
> Proverb 7:4 (NIV)

God's children have wisdom and understanding as family members. Wisdom and understanding do not stand in the dark waiting for you to find them. God gave you wisdom and understanding through Christ. His wisdom includes information for yesterday, today, and tomorrow. Your understanding is complete in Christ. No more wondering if you have all the facts to make a decision. Call on Christ for any decision, and there in lies your wisdom and understanding.

Ask God to show you the facts of any decision that is heavy on your mind. Write out what you hear Him telling you. Ask Him to show you all the facts in this decision.

Patience for Coming Events

At this time, some of you will have your Christmas shopping done, wrapped, and under the tree. Then there are those of us who will have just begun and those who are thinking about getting started. In all of those scenarios, there is one thing that will challenge all of us. That thing is patience! We all have it, but at this time of year, it is usually worn to within an inch of its life and ours. Come with me this week, and give it over to God.

SUNDAY:

> I will praise You, O Lord, with my whole heart; I will tell of all Your marvelous works. I will be glad and rejoice in You; I will sing praise to Your name, O Most High.
>
> Psalm 9:1–2 (NKJV)

Sometimes patience is a hard thing to come by. If in those moments, we can turn our thoughts to our heavenly Father we can transform our minds, and thereby our actions, to being patient. Our thought processes really do control our actions. When you find yourself at an impatient moment, think on God with your whole heart. Remind yourself of Him and all His wonders. Rejoice in His presence.

How can you praise God with your whole heart?

MONDAY:

> I will sing to the Lord, because He has dealt bountifully with me.
>
> Psalm 13:6 (NKJV)

Impatient moments usually come at a time when we have no time. We are full up with to-dos, and the list is getting longer. Seems as though no matter how many items we check off, there have been three more added. Take today, and sing to our Father all He has provided to you. These provisions should include not just the worldly things we must have to live but also the love we have for others and their love returning to us.

Reflect on the love you give to others and what they give back.

TUESDAY:

> That I may proclaim with the voice of thanksgiving, and tell of all Your wondrous works, Lord. I have loved the habitation of Your house, and the place where Your glory dwells.
>
> Psalm 26:7–8 (NKJV)

By proclaiming out loud God's works in our lives we have brought glory to our Father and peacefulness to mind. It only takes a few seconds to say out loud, "Thank you!" for His love toward you. Take a moment; it will do you good.

Journal your thanks to God for His work in you life.

WEDNESDAY:

> Many, O Lord my God, are Your wonderful works which You have done; and Your thoughts toward us cannot be recounted to You in order; if I would declare and speak of them, they are more than can be numbered.
>
> Psalm 40:5 (NKJV)

What God provides is unnumbered and cannot be counted. But we can make a small list. Take some time today, and write a list of what He provides for you each and every day. Then add to that list, things that have been out of the ordinary. Put your list in your billfold or something you carry with you at all times. When stress hits and your patience wanes, pull your list out and read it aloud.

Begin your list in your journal today.

THURSDAY:

> It is good to give thanks to the Lord, and to sing praises to Your name, O Most High; to declare Your loving-kindness in the morning, and Your faithfulness every night … For You, Lord, have made me glad through Your work; I will triumph in the works of Your hands.
>
> Psalm 92:1, 2, 4 (NKJV)

Try this for seven days without missing a day: Before you put your feet on the floor from last nights sleep, tell God thank you. You can either be specific about something or just say a general thank you. Say it out loud, so you actually hear yourself. It does not have to be loud, just verbal. See if it doesn't change your perspective for the coming day's happenings.

Remind your self of a hymn you know by heart, write a few lines below.

FRIDAY:

> Oh, sing to the Lord a new song! For He has done marvelous things; His right hand and His holy arm have gained Him the victory.
>
> Psalm 98:1 (NKJV)

Know any gospel songs by heart? Doesn't matter, make your own. God loves to hear us singing to Him. Your words don't have to rhyme; they just have to be honest. He loves a melody. Your singing to Him will never be out of tune, so don't worry if your bucket isn't nearby. Sing His praises and your questions.

Write a few words to Him now, and then you can use them throughout the day when your patience is at low tide.

SATURDAY:

> Oh, give thanks to the Lord, for He is good! For His mercy endures forever. Oh, give thanks to the God of gods! For His mercy endures forever. Oh, give thanks to the Lord of lords! For His mercy endures forever.
>
> Psalm 136: 1–3 (NKJV)

Mercy is one of God's strong points. Thank Him for that today, and include asking forgiveness for the times you have not been merciful to yourself. The Lord positively loves to forgive you when you ask Him. His mercy endures forever. It only requires your asking.

Remind yourself how God kept you from the cold inside your heart by being with you at every moment.

Flowers in December

December is a month filled with dichotomy. It is a fun month but also busy. The weather can be freezing or sunshine all around. It may be filled with family and friends get-togethers, or it can have some very lonesome days and nights. As I took a few moments to enjoy some silence, I looked out my back window and saw a rose blooming in the middle of December. My first thought was, "I cannot be seeing what I think I see." As I walked to the rose garden, God touched my heart to say, "Yes, no matter what your surroundings, my daughter, I will grow you a beautiful flower."

SUNDAY:

> The Lord of hosts is with us; the God of Jacob is our refuge.
>
> Psalm 46:7 (NKJV)

In our December of *stress,* He grows the flower of *refuge.* Stress is what we bring on ourselves by overloading our bodies with work or our minds with concerns. God promises peace to us if we but breathe His name. Go ahead; today, breathe to Him your stress.

List some of things bringing you stress today, then hand them over to God.

MONDAY:

> You will keep him in perfect peace, whose mind is stayed on You, because he trusts in You.
>
> Isaiah 26:3 (NKJV)

In our December of worry, *He grows the flower of* serenity.

Today's generations are the champions of worry. The majority of us have enough money, housing, and food. We have friends and loved ones, but we still have maximum worries. Take today, and give them all to God. His shoulders can carry all of them.

List some of the things you worry about on a daily basis. Now ask God to bring their end to light.

TUESDAY:

> Peace I leave with you, my peace I give to you; not as the world gives do I give to you. Let not your heart be troubled, neither let it be afraid.
>
> John 14:27 (NKJV)

In our December of frustration, *He grows the flower of* peace.

Frustration comes about when our plans or hopes have gone a different direction than we wanted. In the middle of being frustrated, it really does not matter the why of its misdirection. What matters is, it is not working out! Today, ask God to correct your slightest frustration. He will.

Look back on any situation you felt did not turn out like you thought it should. Now look at how God answered the situation. Do you still feel it didn't end right?

WEDNESDAY:

> Behold, I give you the authority to trample on serpents and scorpions, and over all the power of the enemy, and nothing shall by any means hurt you.
>
> Luke 10:19 (NKJV)

In our December of fatigue, *He grows the flower of* energy.

Fatigue is not just tired. It the last step before collapse. It is physical, mental, and emotional shutdown. Now is the season! Again, we are mostly responsible for doing it to ourselves, but Jesus gives us power over fatigue of any kind. There is no sin in fatigue. Sin enters in when we haven't asked God to supply.

Take time now to ask God to intercede for you rather it is physical, mental, or emotional intervention you need.

THURSDAY:

Cease from anger, and forsake wrath; do not fret, it only causes harm.

Psalm 37:8 (NKJV)

Love never fails.

1 Corinthians 13:8a (NKJV)

In our December of anger, *He grows the flower of* love.

Some of us are very good at not showing our outward anger. This does not mean we do not get angry; it just means we seethe inside. We can get so good at it; we find ourselves physically sick with ulcers or even on our way to a stroke. But if we keep our hearts in a mode of love, we just cannot get very angry for very long.

Ask God to still your heart today and cease any anger you may be feeling.

FRIDAY:

> When you pass through the waters, I will be with you; and through the rivers, they shall not overflow you. When you walk through the fire, you shall not be burned, nor shall the flame scorch you. For I am the Lord your God the Holy One of Israel, your Savior.
>
> Isaiah 43:2–3a (NKJV)

In our December of weakness, *He grows the flower of* strength.

Our weakness may be physical or spiritual. The Lord will handle them all. The trick is to ask Him to help, to turn our weakness over to Him, and to leave it with Him.

Write of a weakness you need to turn over to God. Then turn it over once and for all.

SATURDAY:

Finally, brethren, whatever things are true, whatever things are noble, whatever things are just, whatever things are pure, whatever things are lovely, whatever things are of good report, if there is any virtue and if there is anything praiseworthy, meditate on these things.

Philippians 4:8 (NKJV)

In our December of depression, *He grows the flower of* joy.

Depression can hit hard and fast. It can cause and be caused by anger, fatigue, frustration, stress, worry, and weakness. It can consist of mental abnormalities and physical pain. Dear One, Jesus can change all of this and make you free and joyous once again.

If you are depressed now or ever have been, take time now to ask God to turn it to joy.

Love and Hate—War and Peace

God's Word has a lot to say on these four words. To tell the truth, I knew I would find love, war, and peace in the Bible, but I was totally shocked at how much the Bible had to say about hate. I just didn't remember the Bible using the word hate that often–wrong again, "Oh, one of no remembrance." Hate doesn't just lie still inside us; it grows and grows. It doesn't stop growing until God has taken hold of it. This week we are going to find out how God keeps the hate from making us cold inside and out.

SUNDAY:

> He who hates, disguises it with his lips, and lays up deceit within himself.
>
> Proverbs 26:24 (NKJV)

> But God demonstrates His own love toward us, in that while we were still sinners, Christ died for us.
>
> Romans 5:8 (NKJV)

Today's world is filled with deceit. I just never considered deceit equivalent to hating or even the action of hate. To be deceitful, we have to tell a lie or at least not tell all the truth. Either of those cannot be considered love, so we are actually showing hate or disdain to the individual to whom we have not been honest. God would not, nor has He ever, lied to us. You might not like all He tells you, but it is the truth. He showed His love even while we are sinners. He told us of His love for truth by sending His only Son to die on the cross.

Tell God how it made you feel when someone was deceitful to you. Then pray for them.

MONDAY:

> You shall not hate your brother in your heart. You shall surely rebuke your neighbor, and not bear sin because of him.
>
> Leviticus 19:17 (NKJV)

> The Lord has appeared of old to me, saying: "Yes, I have loved you with an everlasting love; therefore with loving kindness I have drawn you."
>
> Jeremiah 31:3 (NKJV)

Sometimes it is very hard to love our brothers and sisters. One of the ways we do not show our love for both brothers and sisters is by not sharing our love of God and Jesus Christ with them. But God has told us He loves us so much He draws us to Him with loving kindness. Choose someone today to whom you can show loving kindness. By getting closer to them, you can tell them how much God loves them and wants to draw near.

Ask for God's forgiveness for holding a hate in your heart. Then forgive yourself and them if you have cause.

TUESDAY:

> Hatred stirs up strife. But love covers all sins.
>
> Proverbs 10:12 (NKJV)

> For God so loved the world that He gave His only begotten Son, that whoever believes in Him should not perish but have everlasting life."
>
> John 3:16 (NKJV)

How is it we have not figured out on our own that we cause all kinds of problems by hating? Our struggles (strife) today manifest themselves by making us physically, emotionally, and mentally ill. Strife shows up when we argue and struggle with individuals or objects in our everyday lives. The only cure for hate or strife is love like our Father (God) loves us. If He could give away His Son so we could have everlasting life, what are we willing to give to spend eternity with Him?

Ask God today to turn your hate and strife to the love He has given you.

WEDNESDAY:

> The Lord your God, who goes before you, He will fight for you, according to all He did for you in Egypt before your eyes.
>
> Deuteronomy 1:30 (NKJV)

> And the God of peace will crush Satan under your feet shortly. The grace of our Lord Jesus Christ be with you. Amen.
>
> Romans 16:20 (NKJV)

How do we reconcile a God of peace who fights for us? That is definitely a question we can ask, but I believe the thought we should focus on with these scriptures is that God is a God of peace. Because He loves us so much, He will put His peacefulness aside to fight (war) all your battles. You cannot control the war, but He can. All your plans and strategies do not compare to what He will do in any of your wars. We cannot battle Satan without God. Let Him do your battles today and every day. Call out to your seven-star general, Jesus Christ.

Tell your Father of a war you need Him to fight for you. Then thank Him for the grace He has provided you.

THURSDAY:

> You must not fear them, for the Lord your God Himself fights for you.
>
> Deuteronomy 3:22 (NKJV)

> You will keep him in perfect peace, whose mind is stayed on You, because he trusts in You.
>
> Isaiah 26:3 (NKJV)

Deuteronomy is the Lord speaking to Joshua and the battles he is about to do for the promised land. I believe God supplied this scripture for our battles too. We are not to keep our minds (and hearts) on the battles but instead on God. Only then can we find ourselves in perfect peace with God.

Tell God today how much you trust Him to fight your battles and keep you in peace at the same time.

FRIDAY:

Scatter the peoples who delight in war.

Psalm 68:30b (NKJV)

And let the peace of God rule in your hearts, to which also you were called in one body; and be thankful.

Colossians 3:15 (NKJV)

If we delight in war (disruption), God says we are to be scattered (be away from Him). If you delight in Him and His peace, you will be called into His body of believers, and you will be thankful. That sounds pretty easy to understand. Yet in today's world, there is so much strife going on, it is "work" to keep our minds "stayed" on Him. That is one reason to stay in constant contact with God. It is only through daily reading of His word and constant prayer that we can let our hearts be ruled with the peace of God.

Write out today what the 'Peace of God' means to you.

SATURDAY:

> My soul has dwelt too long with one who hates peace. I am for peace; but when I speak, they are for war.
>
> Psalm 120:6–7 (NKJV)

Is there someone in your daily life that thrives on causing disruption? If so, begin praying for them today and continue to pray for them. God can and will change them. We have no way to know someone's situation(s) in life. You cannot change them or even their situations. You can pray for them. You can give them positives where only negatives abide. Ask God to help you each time you are put in their path. He will tell you what to say and how to respond to anything they say or do.

Think of someone you know who is almost always throwing negatives you way. Tell God you need His help in dealing with them.

God's Provision in Your Wilderness

The devotions this week will show when you are in your wilderness, God is with you. He provides for you in your times of need. He will present the pathway out of your wilderness. Take each step with Him, do not run ahead, or even lag behind. Allow Him to be your guide.

SUNDAY:

> By day the LORD went ahead of them in a pillar of cloud to guide them on their way and by night in a pillar of fire to give them light, so that they could travel by day or night. Neither the pillar of cloud by day nor the pillar of fire by night left its place in front of the people.
>
> Exodus 13:21–22 (NIV)

You may be in a wilderness experience right now. God is your guide. Spend time each day with Him in prayer. He will direct your day and night with His light. He is there at all times no matter how dark your wilderness. Look for His light and His light alone.

Write out your wilderness experience below. Ask God to show you the way out of the wilderness and into His light.

MONDAY:

> Do not be afraid. Stand firm and you will see the deliverance the LORD will bring you today … Raise your staff and stretch out your hand over the sea to divide the water so the Israelites can go through the sea on dry ground.
>
> Exodus 14:13a, 16 (NIV)

You may be at a point where you feel your wilderness is swallowing you. Believe the One guiding you will make a path to take you out. He knows where you are. He divided the waters for the Israelites, and He can bring you out of your wilderness. Stretch out your staff (your heart) to Him, and follow on dry ground.

Ask Him to show you the path; cry out from your heart. Tell Him of the sinkingness you feel. Write it out to Him on the lines below. Allow Him to divide your waters in the wilderness.

TUESDAY:

> So the people grumbled against Moses, saying, "What are we to drink?" Then Moses cried out to the LORD and the LORD showed him a piece of wood, he threw it into the water and the water became sweet.
>
> Exodus15: 24–25a (NIV)

If you are at a point in your wilderness where your thirst cannot be quenched, drink of His sweet water. You will never be thirsty if you drink of Him. Today, throw the wood (His Word) into the water where you are drowning and drink. Allow Him to quench your thirst today and every day.

What words of His did He give you that you may drink in today and not be thirsty? Use the area below to thank Him for His words that quench your thirst.

WEDNESDAY:

> Then the Lord said to Moses, "I will rain down bread from heaven for you. The people are to go out each day and gather enough for that day."
>
> Exodus 16:4a (NIV)

God gives you enough to make it through the wilderness day by day, but you should not take more than He offers. He knows your needs. Ask Him for today's portion. He will rain it down on you as you need it.

What is your need for today? Put pen to paper on the lines below to tell Him of your need.

THURSDAY:

> The LORD said to Moses, "I have heard the grumbling of the Israelites. Tell them, 'At twilight you will eat meat, and in the morning you will be filled with bread. Then you will know that I am the LORD your God.'"
>
> Exodus16:11–12 (NIV)

He provides your needs (bread) each day to survive the wilderness. He also makes provisions for your wants (meat). Every day, He rains down the bread and brings the meat to you. Gather the amount needed for the day to continue your path out of the wilderness.

What is your bread and meat that is raining down on you? List them on the lines below.

FRIDAY:

> The LORD said to Moses, "Send some men to explore the land of Canaan, which I am giving to the Israelites"... There they reported to them and to the whole assembly and showed them the fruit of the land ... But the people who live there are powerful, and the cities are fortified and very large.
>
> Numbers 13:1–2, 26b, 28 (NIV)

Do not, as the Israelites did, doubt the fruit He is providing for you. They doubted the Lord and focused on the negatives. Today know He has wonders for you in the new land. Trust Him; walk into the new land He gives you. Taste the fruit of the new land and praise Him for the sweetness of them.

Tell Him of your thankfulness for the new land He is showing you. Use the area below to write out your prayer.

SATURDAY:

> Giving orders to the people: "When you see the ark of the covenant of the LORD your God, and the priests who are Levites, carrying it, you are to move out from your positions and follow it. Then you will know which way to go, since you have never been this way before ..."
>
> Joshua 3:3–4a (NIV)

At the end of your wilderness, watch and follow Him as He leads you out. Since you have not been on this path before follow His lead. Let Him show you a land filled with fruits you cannot imagine. Believe, and follow Him today to your new life.

Give Him your thanks for leading you out of your wilderness. Praise Him for the path He has made clear to you. Use the lines below to write out your prayer.

Keeping Resolutions

It is coming rather we want it to or not: the New Year. Yikes! Where did the last year go? The usual thing at this time of year is to make some New Year resolutions. Granted, very few are kept by the end of January, yet we keep making them. The problem is not in making resolutions; the problem comes when we make one then break it. We are usually left with a feeling of despair or rebuke ourselves for even trying. Let's look at how we can be resolution keepers all year long and how God helps us keep them.

SUNDAY:

Your word is a lamp to my feet and a light to my path.

Psalm 119:105 (NKJV)

It is very hard to see in the dark. If we cannot see the path, how can we make sure we are following the same path day after day? God's word is all the light we ever need. He gives you every answer to all your questions. You only need to ask, believe, and wait for His time to answer. Many of the questions we have can be answered by simply opening His word and reading His answer.

Ask Him today to help you set your list of resolutions for this coming year.

MONDAY:

> Your word I have hidden in my heart that I might not sin against You.
>
> Psalm 119:11 (NKJV)

One of the quickest ways to answer some of your questions is to have God's word stored in your memory banks for recall. Memorizing God's word is not just for making sure we do not sin but also can be used for the pleasure of assisting others. Sometimes just one of God's loving verses will lift your spirit for a week or even longer. Find a verse this week and memorize it, even if it is one just for you.

Write your new memory verse in you journal today.

TUESDAY:

> Grace and peace be multiplied to you in the knowledge of God and of Jesus our Lord … by which have been given to us exceedingly great and precious promises, that through these you may be partakers of the divine nature, having escaped the corruption that is in the world through lust.
>
> 2 Peter 1:2, 4 (NKJV)

Only through the knowledge of God and Jesus can we have peace and it be multiplied. Only by their knowledge and peace should we make our resolutions (changes) for the coming years. Knowledge of God and Jesus comes from His word (Holy Bible) and our personal relationship with them. Think on it this way: how many close friends do you have that you have no knowledge of their convictions or/and with whom you do not have a personal relationship? Bet that answer is none! Begin your resolutions for the year with a conviction to *know* the Father and the Son.

Ask God today to let you know Him in a more personal way.

WEDNESDAY:

> Then Jesus said to those Jews who believed Him, "If you abide in My word, you are My disciples indeed. And you shall know the truth, and the truth shall make you free."
>
> John 8:31–32 (NKJV)

Abiding in God's word means to read it, to feel it, to be convicted by it, and finally, to do it. To make changes in your life does not make sense if you have not consulted the One who loves you enough to tell you the truth in all things. He will guide you in all you do, and that includes resolutions for the coming year. He will assist you in keeping those resolutions. No one else on this planet will personally care, if you keep your resolutions or not. He will. He loves you that much!

Abide in His words today. Ask Him to show you truths you did not know before today.

THURSDAY:

He restores my soul; He leads me in the paths of righteousness for His name's sake.

Psalm 23:3 (NKJV)

So what happens this year if your 'friends' see you break a New Year's Resolution? Nothing, did you say? You are right, but if you make a resolution to your Father, He loves you enough to care if you break it. His caring will restore your soul (forgive you), and He will put you back on the path of righteousness, all because you belong to Him. You are His child (His namesake).

Thank Him today that He cares enough about you to be with you in any changes you want to make in your life.

FRIDAY:

Your testimonies also are my delight and my counselors.

Psalm 119:24 (NKJV)

Know any good counselors or therapists who are free by the hour? Our Holy Father is! The best part is you can call Him any time day or night. He will pick up the phone. He will guide you, and He knows *all* the answers. Take your list of resolutions to Him. Lift them to Him one-by-one. Let Him know by your words what you want to change and ask Him how He wants you to go about making the changes. He will be delighted and will set your anxieties to rest.

Begin your list of resolutions, but wait for God to tell you what they should be. List them today.

SATURDAY:

> This Book of Law shall not depart from your mouth, but you shall meditate in it day and night, that you may observe to do according to all that is written in it. For then you will make your way prosperous, and then you will have good success.
>
> Joshua 1:8 (NKJV)

There is only one book that can promise us prosperity and deliver on that promise. It is God's inspired Word. The promises listed in this verse are more than any of us can ever hope for. You can gain both promises if you go to God daily, night and day. Read His words, meditate on His words, and then do His words. It will not let you down. His promises are made to make you prosperous and give you good success. Neither, of which, has He limited.

Go to chapter 1 of Luke, read it, and meditate on it; then write what it made you think about.

Waiting

Personally, I hate waiting. I am by nature a "do it now" person. But God's timing is not my timing. He knows the perfect time for everything. Over the years I have learned waiting on Him time had kept me from making mistakes I might not have recovered from. The short story is He never left me to rot in the whirl of time. Instead He was right there with me all the time I was in His waiting room.

SUNDAY:

> Wait on the Lord; be of good courage, and He shall strengthen your heart; Wait, I say, on the Lord!
>
> Psalm 27:14 (NKJV)

I have never counted, but I would be willing to claim that I remind myself: "love is patient" at least a thousand times a week. For me to wait on anything for any amount of time is arduous. But God always has good reason for asking us to do anything. Could be we are to wait, because we are not ready, or maybe the "it" is not ready for us. Could be to have "it" now would cause harm, or maybe the "it" just would not be as effective as He wishes according to His plans. So I will continue to remind myself to wait with a glad heart and an even temper, because when "it" arrives, "it" will have all God's blessings attached.

Remind your self today of something you waited for and when "it" arrived "it" was better than you anticipated.

MONDAY:

> My soul, wait silently for God alone, for my expectation is from Him.
>
> Psalm 62:5 (NKJV)

What are you waiting for today? Maybe a promotion, a letter, a raise, an understanding of someone or something that has happened in the past is what would set your mind at ease. Scripture tells us we actually wait with our soul. That tells me why waiting patiently is very important to us as individuals. By setting my wants aside and realizing my waiting is really from Him and not because of Him, I can now expect only the best. God does not pass out anything, if it is not worth having.

Write to Him about what you are waiting for.

TUESDAY:

Our soul waits for the Lord; He is our help and our shield.

Psalm 33:20 (NKJV)

If waiting is as hard for you as it is for me, think on the scripture above. While we are required to wait for many things in our daily lives, we are always shielded with God's love and help. A shield of any kind is for your protection and comfort. You have not been afforded a manmade shield but instead the covering of God Himself. Your protection or shield will cover every need. Thank God today for His help and shield whenever you must wait.

Write your thanks to Him personally.

WEDNESDAY:

> I wait for the Lord, my soul waits, and in His word I do hope.
>
> Psalm 130:5 (NKJV)

Did you realize our hope comes from waiting? I cannot ever remember putting hope and waiting in the same breath. The scripture tells us hope comes from waiting on the Lord. If we believe God is good and His love comes to us daily, then we must believe what He has asked us to wait on must be good and filled with His love. Praise Him today for being in all your waiting moments.

What does now knowing your hope comes from waiting bring to mind?

THURSDAY:

> Let us hold fast the confession of our hope without wavering, for He who promised is faithful.
>
> Hebrews 10:23 (NKJV)

"Holding fast" indicates there is a time of waiting. This scripture tells us we are to wait without wavering. Wavering is to question the good or evil of a waiting situation. But God is faithful always, so it only stands to reason He will be faithful in our waiting. If we spend our waiting time making our own scenarios of how things will turn out, we are not waiting without wavering. You must confess to God that you are totally dependent on His decisions in your waiting. Thank Him for His love, patience, and control in all your waiting.

FRIDAY:

> The eyes of all look expectantly to You, and You give them their food in due season, You open Your hand and satisfy the desire of every living thing.
>
> Psalm 145:15–16 (NKJV)

We can expect God to answer our every need, and that includes our times of waiting. God provided food, shelter, and water to the Israelites when they crossed the desert, so why do we not allow Him to answer our call when we are waiting. Their manna was given daily in the exact right amounts. If they took more than they ate that day, the manna was spoiled when they awakened. The same is true with our waiting. If we jump ahead of God's plan, our ending will be spoiled. It will not be in His perfect plan. Wait. You will be satisfied with your desires.

Look expectantly to your Lord today, and write about your satisfaction to your desires.

SATURDAY:

> For the vision is yet for an appointed time; But at the end it will speak, and it will not lie. Though it tarries, wait for it; because it will surely come, it will not tarry.
>
> Habakkuk 2:3 (NKJV)

This scripture is filled with so many promises straight from God. Whatever we are waiting for and for however long we must wait, there is an appointed time. God Himself will reward our waiting. It is His vision we are waiting for, always. Wait. It will not tarry.

Tell yourself some things you might do while you are waiting on God's timing.

Safe in His Arms

I have a favorite picture of my daddy. It is a picture of me as a child in his arms. When I look at it, I see a warm smile on his face and a secure grin on mine. I enjoy looking back and remembering, not just my childhood, but last year, last month, and even last week. There is no need for me to feel despair. Even though my earthly father has gone on to be with the Lord, I know I am not left out in the cold for I can always remember whatever my situation, I am safe in my Father's arms. Utilize this week's daily devotional to remind you that you are safe as well.

SUNDAY:

> Glory ye in his holy name: let the heart of them rejoice that seek the LORD. Seek the LORD and his strength; seek his face continually. Remember his marvelous works that he hath done, his wonders, and the judgments of his mouth.
>
> 1 Chronicles 16:10–12 (KJV)

A favorite song of mine is "You Alone" written by Echoing Angels. The first words tell of one "Desperately wanting to just find a way / Searching and seeking for someone to say / That it is alright and it is okay." Listening farther to the song, you realize that this person has found that Jesus *alone* is *God.* Verse 11 above tells to "seek the LORD," seek His strength and His face continually. You may not get the approval your flesh desires, but the soul can be filled with God's love. What things are drawing you to the desperate and lonely way? Give them over to God.

MONDAY:

> But if from thence thou shalt seek the LORD thy God, thou shalt find him, if thou seek him with all thy heart and with all thy soul.
>
> Deuteronomy 4:29 (KJV)

The verse says, "From thence," which means from a previous place or time. "That place" can be your desperate search for safety, or it can be your cold and lonely feeling of hopelessness. By seeking with your whole heart and soul, you can find God. Once found, you can rest in His arms. Your soul is full when you are dwelling with Jesus.

TUESDAY:

He shall enter into peace: they shall rest in their beds.

Isaiah 57:2a (KJV)

In the second verse of "You Alone," "I close my eyes and drift away to somewhere I remember—to a place I feel safe—I am in your arms." Have you ever closed your eyes and drifted away? Tired, sad, worried, wounded, and lonely, wanting to be held, wanting to feel secure? Drift into the love of Jesus Christ, and rest in His arms. Close your eyes and drift into the secure and hope-filled love Jesus gives.

WEDNESDAY:

> Therefore if any man be in Christ, he is a new creature: old things are passed away; behold, all things are become new.
>
> 2 Corinthians 5:17 (KJV)

Sometimes we long for acceptance. God's Word tells us that Jesus forgives, and He accepts us as we are, something few others do. He gives you a clean slate to begin life anew. When winter comes to an end, the snow melts and gives way to new birth. Trust in God, and become new.

THURSDAY:

> To know wisdom and instruction; to perceive the words of understanding.
>
> Proverbs 1:2 (KJV)

The song, "You Alone" ends with, "You love me/And want me to understand that you alone are God." To understand is to "appreciate, value, and identify with." When you feel *no one* cares, know that God *cares.* Snow is beautiful, but it has to be cold outside or the snow melts. To understand and identify with God you must, at times, go through some cold and bleak times. Remember the Words of Christ—he will never forsake you.

FRIDAY:

And ye shall be my people, and I will be your God.

Jeremiah 30:22 (KJV)

Wanting something does not give you satisfaction. Satisfaction is only realized when the "want" becomes "possession." This possession is two sided: He possesses you, and you possess *Him.* Only God completely satisfies. Let Him satisfy you today. Open your heart to Him. Let our shivering and cold soul be warmed by His fireplace of peace and love.

SATURDAY:

> O come, let us worship and bow down: let us kneel before the LORD our maker.
>
> Psalm 95:6 (KJV)

Ending the week with worship brings pleasure as well as excitement. Deepen your relationship with Christ by worshiping Him in praise, song, and prayer. Your strength may be weak and your heart broken and lonely but rest in the arms of Jesus Christ. As you kneel before Him today, relax in the fact that you are *safe* in *His arms.*

about the authors

Kathleen Jones was eight years old when she accepted Christ as her Savior. As a wife and mother, she is often accused of "mothering" all with which she spends time. Current activities in her local church include teaching adult Bible studies, being a deacon, and being missions' team leader. When God impressed upon her to do a devotions book, she did not come to His understandings immediately. Because she knows God loves her (and you) so sincerely, He has taught her to communicate His Words for daily life.

Maureen Eubank became a believer at the age of fourteen at a church summer camp. As a wife, mother, step-mother, and grandmother, she has a passion for women to know the Father intimately. For over ten years, she has been involved in all types of Women's Ministries. Bible study groups for women have met in her home. Knowing her own daily devotions have brought her to a greater understanding of the great "I AM," she could not help but say yes to Peggy and Kath when the book adventure began.

Peggy Seay accepted salvation through Jesus Christ in her late twenties. Yes, they are all sisters—in Christ and biologically. Peggy is a wife, mother, and grandmother. Leading Bible studies has been a part of her life for over twenty years. The age groups included toddlers through pre-college. She and her husband directed and worked with at-risk youth for over four years. She continually builds her intimate relationship with Jesus Christ by her own daily devotional studies. She enjoys finding Christ and learning life-lessons each day. Whether reading a book, listening to music, watching a movie or TV, or simply exploring nature, you can be sure God will touch your personal life if you open the door to your heart and mind.